UNTIL I DIE

Until I Die
Copyright © 2023
Beverly ND Clopton

ISBN: 978-1-957344-59-1

Cover concept and design by Mike Parker

Published by WordCrafts Press
Cody, Wyoming 82414
www.wordcrafts.net

UNTIL I DIE

Reflections and Tales

BEVERLY ND CLOPTON

WordCrafts Press

In Memory of My Sister
Christa RD Burrows

CONTENTS

The title of this book sprang to mind immediately when I decided I wanted to write book number five. I liked it. The idea of writing until I am unable to write anymore because I cease to exist seemed a natural fit for someone who loves word crafting. But then those imps who plague writers by sprinkling doubt or uncertainty found a loophole, and I had second thoughts. Was the title a little too somber? Perhaps something like "In His Company" might be more fitting for a collection of reflective essays written to inspire, inform, and challenge Christian believers of this astonishing time in our history. During one of my virtual visits with my adult son, who resides in a skilled nursing/rehab facility because of a stroke that felled him some years ago, I asked his opinion. Though he requires skilled nursing care, is paralyzed and unable to speak clearly, his mind was untouched by the stroke. Cognitively, he's as sharp as he always was. I shared my indecision about the title and asked him to weigh in. Holding up the two titles, I asked which I should use. He shook his head "No" to *In His Company* and "Yes" to *Until I Die*. I smiled. Perhaps his situation weighed in; I don't know; but I felt and still feel the title is a natural follow up to *Rigors of the Call*, my book that preceded this one.

I have come to understand that not only is God's call rigorous, it is forever. He created us to worship Him from the moment we are aware of His existence in our mortal form until we come into His presence in our heavenly one. What He purposes for us in our expressions of that worship is not something to pick up or put down whenever we feel like it. No, our worship, our being about His business is for always—until we die. So, I pen these reflections and tales of varying subjects and experiences, because I feel He designed me to do that. In worship of Him, I write until I die.

CHAPTER 1

THE URGENCY OF NOW
(2020)

U rgency is defined as something that requires swift or fast action; something that is insistent, that demands immediate attention else it causes harm. We live now in such a moment; an unprecedent period in our history that threatens who we are and who God calls us to be. It is a moment of urgency that forces us to examine who we were, who we are, and who we aspire to be as people of faith in a nation experiencing not *the best of times*, but *the worst of times*. The author of 2 Chronicles, in chapter 7, verses 14–15, offers the remedy for addressing this urgency of our current epoch.

> *"If my people who are called by my name, will humble themselves and pray and seek my face and turn from their wicked ways, then I will hear from heaven and will forgive their sin and will heal their land. Now my eyes will be open and my ears attentive to the prayers offered in this place."*

Perhaps the best way to avail ourselves of this promise is by beginning at the beginning. As Americans, we are not often characterized as a *humble* people. Our heralded successes as the most powerful nation in the Western World have not inspired a national sense of humility. Quite the contrary. We are a proud and ofttimes arrogant people; confident in our standing on the world stage. But that image of who we are as a people is tainted. It has been applicable only to those of European descent, excluding all others, and most especially those whose ancestors were brought to the shores on slave ships and sold as property. For 244 years our nation has wrestled with the conundrum of a race-based caste society. It remains an existential issue and highlights the urgency of the times. Underlying the current racial justice pandemic sweeping throughout the land is this very issue. Looking in the mirror and owning the reality of the truth of social justice movements like Black Lives Matter has become as urgent for the nation as its ongoing battle against the viral pandemic of coronavirus. Both pandemics, one physical, one social and spiritual, force us to this examination.

Since the beginning of 2016, we have grappled with the unraveling of the many of the principles that undergird our democratic form of government. This assault upon those ideals (admittedly not always implemented for all the people, but there nonetheless for implementation) has brought us to the urgency of now. As the nation continues to witness the fraying of the fabric of the beliefs that bind us together as one people by men and women of ill-repute, unqualified for the positions they hold, immoral in words and deeds, we stand now with the guiding words of scripture: embrace humility, pray, seek God's face, and turn from our wicked ways. This is the swift action needed to address the urgency of now.

Throwing off the mantle of pride, arrogance, superiority, and race privilege is not easy. One must first acknowledge wearing it. For those who have done so for many years, it is an invisible cloak, and to look in the mirror and say to oneself, *"Yes, I have benefitted by being of my race. I have internalized attitudes and postures without realizing that they are indicative of privilege based on accident of birth,"* requires a humble spirit. But such an acknowledgement individually and collectively is the first step in quashing the mantle's influence. When humility is a definer of who you are, praying seems to spring up with little effort. Humility forces an inward look and realization that only by God's grace are we able to be who He created us to be. That realization leads almost immediately to prayer; to expressions of thanksgiving to the God who has allowed us to have, to do, to be. As we become humbler, more prayerful, we become seekers after this God who has done and is doing so much in our lives. We want to know Him better; we turn to His written word to do that. It is within that divinely inspired book that we come face to face with the wickedness of our ways. That awareness is the impetus to turn away from what we have discovered about ourselves, that keeps God's face turned from us. It is in the moment of turning away from wickedness and turning to God that His promise is activated.

This is where we stand in the United States of America this August of 2020—a viral pandemic still having its deadly sway—a social justice pandemic under attack for suggesting that the country is not fine as it is—an impending election that will determine the fate of a nation from whom God has turned His face. "*It is the worst of times.*" We are on a precipice from which we may fall headlong into further alienation from our heavenly Father if we fail to heed the warnings. Yet, there remains time to begin the correction of our sinful ways; to change direction and begin to navigate a new course. It goes without saying that the adage credited to Albert Einstein: "*The definition of insanity is doing the same thing over and over again, but expecting different results,*" is worthy of note. To keep doing what scripture informs us is not what God wants us to do, expecting that He will fulfill a promise, is insanity. We must exercise our rights as citizens to move the dial from insanity by turning out an administration that is unworthy of the trust of the people and beginning a course with one more suited to the demands of governing and more importantly to the demands of God. The time for change is upon us. This is the urgency of now. When I look backward some time from now, may I see we did not fail to take the quick and sure action to forestall further disaster.

CHAPTER 2

THE SOUL OF A NATION

Does a nation have a soul? Within its collective construct of people of varying ethnic and religious backgrounds, of skin tones across the color spectrum and cultural experiences stretching north to south, east to west, can it be said of such a body that it has a soul? Unequivocally I answer, "yes." The soul of this nation was fashioned by the concepts and beliefs that formed it. Primary among them was the belief that all people are created equal irrespective of race or ethnic origin, that they have the fundamental rights of liberty, free speech, religious freedom, freedom of assembly, and the due process of law. From a theological perspective, the soul is an ethereal spirit or driving force within an individual. It's the *oil* that lubricates mankind's inner being. Underpinning the national soul is a similar construct. The force that drives us as a people is the soul of our belief systems. Right now, in this time, our soul is under attack. We have not faced such a threat to the design of our democratic form of government on our own soil since the Civil War. Henry David Thoreau's words penned in the 1800s resonate for us today: "What lies behind us and what lies ahead of us are tiny matters compared to what lives within us." For what lives within us defines who we are as a people, and who we are as a people speaks by our actions to our souls.

For almost four years, we the people have lived in unimaginable times. We have watched as evil has had its sway; as efforts to weaken the written precepts of our constitution and Bill of Rights have grown. We have bemoaned attempts to circumvent and even destroy laws passed in prior administrations for the welfare of the people. We have watched race baiting and increasing racial divides edged on by authorities out of step with the constitution and the word of God. We have grown accustomed to a president who fabricates without second thought and who doesn't seem to care that the untruths are recorded and documented; that everyone knows that he is a liar. We have lamented as the least qualified receive governmental political appointments, and stood in mute disbelief at the life-long appoint- ments of partisan judges to our nation's highest court. When we thought it could get no worse, it did. A black man was killed in full view of cameras by a white policeman who ignored his own officers' attempts to stop him; and a viral pandemic hit the continental shores of the nation bringing it to its knees in a matter of months. Both incidents sparked flames that simmered beneath the surface of the national facade of American greatness.

With national crises demanding real leadership thrust upon him, the "Make America Great Again" president revealed what lays within him. Nothing. Thus with no one to lead, to unify the nation across its multi-faceted character, to help it embrace its highest founding principles and to seek solace in its spiritual foundations, to encour- age it to follow the wisdom of the scientific community, a nation desperate for guidance has been forced to look beyond its elected leadership. It has turned its eyes inward, reaching into its soul for guidance. No, it is not yet a consortium of all of us, but more and more of us are remembering our Judeo-Christian theologies; more and more are looking back at past movements that fostered positive changes; more and more are examining themselves and acknowledg- ing that what the nation has become is neither what it was founded to be, nor what they want it to be.

We the people stand at a moral and spiritual crossroad. Two improbable juxtaposed moments—a yet uncontrolled viral pandemic and a demand for social justice in situations where it is still denied- have morphed into a soul-defining movement. It is a movement that will lay bare who we are as a people of faith. Our heritage and beliefs speak to what the God we profess has said to His people in soul-defining moments such as these. Down through the ages until just such a time as this, the choice has been ours to either live those beliefs or reject them to our peril. We are wise to recall the words of Hebrews 4:12-13:

> *"For the word of God is alive and active. Sharper than any double-edged sword, it penetrates even to dividing soul and spirit, joints and marrow; it judges the thoughts and attitudes of the heart. Nothing in all creation is hidden from God's sight. Everything is uncovered and laid bare before the eyes of him to whom we must give account."*

And Deuteronomy 6:5:

> *"Love the Lord your God with all your heart and with all your soul and with all your strength."*

These scriptures speak to our current crises. If we indeed will love Him as His word so directs; and believe that He is omnipotent and omnipresent, the soul of our nation will survive this attempt by the enemy to destroy it. The spiritual and moral foundation is laid. We have but to build upon it. May God so speak to our hearts and minds this November that we chose to begin the healing of the character of this nation by turning away from the ruin of the past four years, and those responsible for it.

CHAPTER 3

Is God in the Pandemics?

When life throws curve balls, dropped passes, and shots that bounce off the rim; when our plans are forestalled, our dreams dashed and our efforts come to naught, the initial reaction is to cry out to God—whether we profess Him or not—and in utter frustration, lament, "*O, God, why is this happening to me? Where are you?*" That reaction is nothing new. Since recorded time, humankind has spoken similar words whenever the ugliness of life intrudes and destroys the perception of its beauty. The psalmist David most accurately captured that feeling of despair when life is off-kilter, and we are lost without answers or seeming recourse. Thousands of years ago, he wrote, "*My God, my God, why have you forsaken me? Why are you so far from saving me, so far from my cries of anguish? My God, I cry out by day, but you do not answer, by night, but I find no rest.*" (Psalm 22:1-2, [NRSV]) Today around the world as people who know God and His Son Jesus as our Savior, we identify with that anguish as we grapple with a viral pandemic that has brought unrelenting illness and death. And here in the United States, we face a two-edged sword: both a viral pandemic and a social injustice pandemic shatter the norms of the land. The façade of "*America the Beautiful*" is stripped away and an ugly underbelly, long glossed over with a veneer of democracy, exposes itself.

One is tempted to think that God would have spared us—His people of a Judeo-Christian nation—that we would, with the rest of the world, be contending only with the viral pandemic that so far outwits us and wreaks havoc at will. Surely, the desperate search for medicinal and therapeutic remedies is enough of a challenge. But that is not the reality of the moment. We stand in this period of history confronted with the fact that life in America is undeniably changed. There will be no turning back the clock to the days of old. We watch the daily numbers on the sidebar of the television screen, and the COVID-19 illnesses and deaths they represent are likely seared into our consciousness forever. We continue to battle the pandemic of racial privilege and social injustice and the current efforts to deny political justice to people of color as we move closer to national elections in November. Our sense of what it means to be American is being shaped by these pandemics. And if that is the case, I shout a resounding "YES" to the question of this piece: Is God in the Pandemics?

We people of faith believe God is omnipotent, omnipresent and omniscient; translation: He is all-powerful; He is everywhere at the same time; He is all-knowing. This belief system allows us to understand Him in ways that are foreign to those who don't. We know He knew this viral pandemic was coming; at the founding of this nation, He knew that the question of race would still be the "thorn in its side" in the Year of the Lord, 2020. We know that God is no promoter of evil, but just the opposite, a champion of good. But we also acknowledge that as He works to achieve that good in the lives of a rebellious people, His processes for their deliverance and salvation come with a price.

Consider for a moment the biblical saga of Joseph, the favored son of Jacob sold into Egyptian slavery by his brothers. In what would normally be a tale that ended in sorrow and grief, it is instead one that testifies to God's omniscience and omnipotence. Rather than withering away in prison, Joseph rises to power in the realm of his capturers: *"So Pharaoh said to Joseph, 'I hereby put you in charge of the whole land of Egypt.'"* (Genesis 41:41) In that position of authority, Joseph, because of God's plans revealed to him in visions, is able to save the lives not only of Egyptians, but those of his family, the Israelites. The very brothers who sold him away those many years ago now bow at his feet seeking food for themselves and families as a famine sweeps the land. Joseph reveals his identity and tells his brothers that what they had intended by their deed was not God's plan. Joseph explains that it was not them who sent him to Egypt, but God; that God placed him in his present position so that he could save their lives and preserve them as a remnant on earth. (Genesis 45) Such a story from the holy word that guides our beliefs offers us an assurance during this unprecedented time in modern history. It reminds us that pandemics like famines are within His power to control. His knows their purpose. His presence is within them. And so too with the social justice ills that continue to plague us. The moment the first slaves were captured and shipped to this and other countries some 400 plus years ago did not come as a surprise to God. He foreknew the sin that authored such depravity would lay waste and ravish humanity. But as with Joseph's bondage, He continues to use what humans mean for evil in the realm of social inequality and injustice to bring about His will and purposes. Yes, in this social pandemic it seems the wait for its cure has been unbearably long. We yearn for its eradication as eagerly as we do for that of the viral pandemic.

We find hope on both fronts as we see Him at work, giving wisdom and discernment to those in the scientific community. We know without His input their ideas and efforts will be to no avail. They will labor in vain unless He gives the cerebral spark that leads them in the direction He purposes. Oh, they may not own that, or even believe in His ability to so do. But we of faith know; nothing occurs unless it passes first by Him for approval. We know that what may seem negative experiences to us will have consequences beyond our limited minds to process; that such consequences may not even be seen in our lifetimes; but they will fulfill ultimately His designs. We believe that the barriers that serve to block social justice for God's beloved community will not forever stand. His presence will stir the hearts and minds of more and more people; they will awaken to His spirit moving in them, opening their eyes to visions He gives them. The outcries and protests that have arisen nationwide against this social pandemic will not magically cease. In one form or another they will continue until social injustice for all is eradicated and systemic racism becomes but a footnote in the chronicles of the land. As with every generation, He will raise up those, often the least likely among us to lead us in the direction He would have us go. Yes, even during these very difficult times; times when life is ugly and hard and despairing and frightening, the God we know and serve is amongst us. Has He not told us He will never leave nor forsake us? We have His word—one we can take to the bank. Even the psalmist himself eventually admitted there was no reason for his soul to be downcast, despite the circumstances in which he found himself. Let us recall his words as we ride out the ups and down of the current pandemics, confident that God is with us.

"Why, my soul are you downcast? Why so disturbed in me? Put your hope in God, for I will yet praise him, my Savior and my God."
~Psalm 42:5

CHAPTER 4

WHERE ARE THE PROPHETS?

"We are given no miraculous signs; no prophets are left..."
~Psalm 74:9

Thus penned by one Asaph, a singer or musician at the temple in Jerusalem during the Old Testament era, these words speak to the Israelites' plight during their time of exile in Babylonia. It is a lament that asked a heart-wrenching question: Where were God's prophets, the ones who had contact with Him and who brought His words of comfort and hope? The ones who could offer wisdom to sustain them? Though it had been close to 1,500 years since the time of those ancient people's nation—defining exile, I think the question is relevant to us in 2020 AD. The Hebrew word for prophet means "one who is inspired by God." The contemporary dictionary defines it as "a person regarded as an inspired teacher or proclaimer of the will of God; a person who foretells or predicts what is to come." Both definitions are suited to our journey during a time when we, like the exiled Israelites, are desperate for wisdom, for direction, for a word from on high uttered by one inspired by the One who sits high and looks low.

Biblical history informs us that 400-plus years expired between the time of the writings of the last of the Old Testament prophets and the unfolding of events in the New Testament. It has been said that during those 400 years of prophetic silence, it was as if God closed heaven's doors and withdrew from all He had created. Though accounts of who wrote what and when in the times drawing close to that period of darkness are inconclusive, the prophet Malachi is thought to be the last of the known prophets to proclaim, "*Thus says the Lord*," before the celestial shutdown. Tracing backwards from this last prophetic voice to earlier in biblical history when prophets often rose "from the ranks of the people," (Quotes from Harper's Bible Dictionary) individuals such as Amos, Elijah, Jeremiah, and Daniel to name but a few, felt God calling them to speak truth to people of their times regarding issues of morality and religion. They felt an urgency to share the guidance and wisdom God prompted within them. Seemingly sparked by the Holy Spirit their prophetic voices rang out, beseeching their contemporaries to heed God's laws and commandments, especially those decrees related to caring for the poor, the alien, and the downtrodden. They raised their voices against corruption, avarice, pride, idolatry, and self-aggrandizement in secular and sacred institutions. They were unafraid of reprisal and stood rooted in their sense of right and wrong within the context of their faith. They understood that "tomorrow is inherent in today," and were able to forecast the likely outcomes of Israel's continued willful disobedience and "evil pattern of living." (Quotes from Harper's Bible Dictionary)

We of the 21st century living in a nation some 6,744 miles away from the land of the Bible which produced prophets are at a crucial period in history. We have been for some time. For 244 years and counting, we the people whose ancestors founded this country with underlying Christian principles, are faced, as were the Israelites, with social, political, and spiritual conundrums. But unlike them, at present anyway, we have few if any prophets. There is no Isaiah, Jeremiah, or Ezekiel; no Amos, Hosea, Micah, Zechariah, Malachi, no Daniel. For a very brief period some 50 to 60 years ago, some "rose from the ranks of the people"—Howard Thurman, Fannie Lou Hammer, Martin Luther King, Jr—spring to mind, raising their voices to speak to issues of racism, poverty, and other social injustices. But those voices are silent now. Oh, I realize that the times are different; the issues more complex; that successes in some areas give false impressions and foster the belief that overall things are all right with us. But we know better; and we especially know better now—in the United States of America in 2020 AD. In a time of evil gone wild, of lies spoken as truth, of denial of rights and violence against people, especially Black men, gone amok, we long for a prophetic word to galvanize us, to pivot us away from what will eventually destroy the principles of our democracy, to proclaim words and truths that heal and restore and reunite. Whether from a pulpit or a factory floor or an intensive care ward or a fledging campaign office or the planning space of a youth-led protest, our nation needs prophetic voices. For almost four years, it's as if we have lived as did our biblical ancestors for 400 years, with no word from on high. Where are the prophets of our time? Have they run away like Jonah? Have they countered the Holy Spirit's promptings with: "I'm too young; too old; unqualified, uneducated, inexperienced." "I can't speak in public." "I don't have time." "Isn't that the preacher's job?" "Nobody's going listen to what I have to say." "Things aren't that bad; this too will pass." Where are the prophets? Can anyone tell me where they are?

CHAPTER 5

An Unopened Bible
A Parable

In an unidentified time, a black leather-bound Bible of unknown translation sat upon a table. What stirred it suddenly to an awareness of itself remains a mystery. It had rested unopened on a side table in one room or another for as long as it could recall. It did remember being wrapped in festive paper and presented at a family gathering to a young man not yet in his teens as a gift to mark some special occasion. As the young man grew, he kept the Bible in the box which housed it; and though he never opened it, the Bible held significance. That was obvious as times passed and the young man discarded other personal objects that lost their attraction; all except his Bible. It remained; unopened, but there in its box on a table. In silence it watched as its owner passed from puberty into young adulthood; and finally, into full adult status. *Maybe now* the unopened Bible reasoned, as the man matured, *he would open it and embrace what lay upon its pages.* But alas, such was not the case. Gradually it came to be that whenever its owner sat down with some other book, the Bible felt itself stirring with a pang of remorse. It knew the glory of the words on its pages; that they had been inspired by God and composed by those He chose to write them. It understood it was a sacred book; was indeed the most widely read book in the world. And as another night's darkness would surrender to the dawn of light heralding a new day, the unopened Bible wondered, "What must I do to be opened and read like the books lining the bookshelves or sprawled upon tables?"

One day the Bible's owner returned after being away for some time. Throwing open the door, he lifted a woman in his arms and carried her across the threshold. He had married, and the joy of it lit both their faces. Their obvious love for one another filled the room with a sense of promise. The unopened Bible felt a different stirring. *Perhaps now*, it thought, *I will be noticed*. Perhaps the wife knew of it and would be the one to finally take it from its box.

Days turned to weeks and weeks to months, but the Bible stayed unopened in its place on the side table. One day the man's parents came to visit the newly-wed couple. As they sat in the dwindling daylight, after having enjoyed and praised the wife's first solo dinner preparations, the man's mother noticed the Bible.

"Oh my," she said. "Is that the Bible we gave you all those years ago?"

"Yes," the man answered with a somewhat sheepish look, as he anticipated his mother's next question.

"It looks as if you've never taken it out of its box. Have you ever read it?"

The man and his wife looked at each other, remembering the few times since their marriage when they had stopped to glance at the Bible, commenting that one day they really needed to read it, or at least one of them should; and share with the other what it said. Of course, the man felt guilty; after all, the Bible was a gift of pride and tradition given to each child in his family. He knew what it meant to his parents; recalled they read it daily when he was growing up. But over the years as he matured and became more worldly, reading it slipped into one of those things he'd get around to someday when he had more time.

Nothing more was said about the unopened Bible as the evening drew to a close, and the couples said their good-byes. His mother decided she'd bide her time before raising the issue again. She'd grown accustomed to the modern idea of "staying in your lane," and knew an opportune time would present itself again. Unlike the son, she'd lived long enough to appreciate that life's trials and tribulations sooner or later drew one to the only available source for answers, comfort, hope and peace—the Word of God.

As the years continued, the young couple decided it was time to begin a family of their own. They had achieved success in their chosen careers; their home showcased artifacts bought during their travels. They were ready to share their love and joy with little images of themselves. Throughout the years of getting to that point, the Bible had kept its spot on a side table. The couple's busy lives never gave time to opening it; even though they didn't neglect it from a physical perspective. Along with all the décor items on display throughout their home, the Bible was dusted and kept presentable, unopened in its box.

As life would have it, one afternoon as the wife was driving home from a prenatal doctor's appointment, a drunk driver sideswiped her car. She lost control, and although her seat belt kept her from being thrown from the vehicle, she was crushed by the impact of the exploding airbag. Not only did she lose the baby, but her lower pelvic area was severely damaged; and she was paralyzed from the waist down. Needless to say, the devastation that set upon the young couple was overwhelming. Well-wishes and all the other expressions of sympathy and support did little to relieve their anguish and despair. His mother suggested that it was a good time for him to take his Bible out of its box and read some of the scriptures written for times like those. She even sent him specific ones to get started and reminded him that the Bible was divinely inspired and written to be read. So distraught was the couple that the mother's words went unheeded. Nevertheless, she prayed daily that her son would one day find solace in God's word.

Helplessly, the unopened Bible watched as one day bled into the next and his owner moved listlessly through his new normal. How it longed to speak directly to him in this time of devastation and pain. The man had begun to drink more than he did before the accident. One evening as he bumbled his way through the room in which the Bible rested, he bumped into the table. The impact was such that it knocked the Bible onto the floor. As it fell, it was as if its words *"For the word of God is living and active..."* (Hebrews 4:12) came to life in the room; and the Holy Book seized its moment. Tumbling from the box that had held it for so many years, it hit the floor with pages splayed. Stooping to pick it up, the man's eyes fell upon the open pages of the Bible. Staring at him was the 23rd Psalm. As he read silently, he remembered those words from the days of his youth. He recalled the pastor saying the Book of Psalms was the "go to" scripture for words of comfort and encouragement when life took a deep dive into despair. Slowly he began turning the pages, reading, skipping around the passages, pausing at those that seemed to speak to his sorrow and pain. Can an inanimate object be ecstatic? Most will say "No." But the inanimate Bible is the Word of God. And ecstatic doesn't begin to describe the joy felt by this unopened Bible that was finally opened. No matter that it did not physically open itself. The Word of God it contained was *"living and active;"* it was *"sharper than any double-edged sword, it penetrates even to dividing soul and spirit, joints and marrow; it judges the thoughts and attitudes of the heart."* And the Bible, finally opened, proceeded to do just that. The man and his wife discovered they had the antidote for their sorrow at their fingertips all along. They had only to open its pages to assuage the pain and find hope for the future.

It is common knowledge that the Protestant Bible (the Bible of this parable), since its publication in 1611 continues to hold the distinction of being the best-selling book of all times. Writer James Chapman contends over 3.9 billion copies have been sold during the past 50 years. Juxtapose that number with the reported 2.2 billion people world-wide who profess Christianity; that's a Bible in each of their hands, with 1.7 billion copies left over for the agnostics, the atheists, the curious. If we judge its popularity by its sales statistics, we can assume that billions of people have read the Bible; their reasons for doing so varying, but they know its content, and what it purports and teaches. Unfortunately, that assumption would be ill-founded as our parable of an unopened Bible revealed. The harsh and perhaps uncomfortable truth is that the number of Bibles purchased does not inform us of how many of them are actually opened and read. Many a residence possesses a Bible that rests somewhere in the confines of the home, unopened, unread. As our little parable shows, often it is only when trials and tribulations come that we turn to it, embracing the purposes for which it was written. Think of how much of sorrow's sting the young couple might have avoided if reading their Bible had been routine; its wisdom and guidance planted in their hearts for life's uncertainties?

The lesson: God's Word, the Bible—the best selling book in the world—was written to be opened, read, and obeyed; not owned and unopened. And it most certainly was not written to serve as a hand-held prop by a president who neither opened nor read it, in front of a church during a political photo op. The latter scenario will be recorded by history as an example of the Bible's wisdom wasted upon fools.

CHAPTER 6

ANCHORS OF FAITH

I seldom miss the annual broadcast of the National Memorial Day observance in the nation's capital. Among my favorite segments is the roll call of the branches of the armed services. Representatives of each march onto the stage as the anthem that identifies them plays. *"Anchors Aweigh, my boys, anchors aweigh..."* rings as the United States Navy, resplendent in white uniforms, takes its place; their song's lyrics reminding us that anchors are crucial to the performance of their service. When the time comes to cast off, to face the challenges required of them, the sailors raise their anchors to clear the sea bed. In fact, anyone who sails knows a boat without an anchor is useless. Without them—as most vessels have at least two if not more—it would be impossible to keep the boat in place when docked or steer it during bad weather.

The word anchor also has meaning beyond its nautical reference. In its more generic sense, it is used to describe someone who is "a reliable or principal support" and "something that serves to hold an object firmly." All of these definitions support my contention that "faith" has anchors; that our understanding of this primary under-pinning of our spiritual beliefs is supported by them. And that just as secular anchors secure a docked vessel or assist it out in open waters, our faith anchors keep us firmly attached to and supported by the God in whom we live and have our being. We may not have an annual observance whereby we march in fancy uniforms to the rhythm of a catchy anthem, but we do have the stirring lyrics of an old gospel song that identifies us as representatives of the Lord's armed services. *"My soul has been anchored in the Lord."* This sense of a spiritual grounding or anchor upon which believers can cling is the same as the ship captain's dependence upon his man-made anchors; with the exception that our anchor is the Word of God as revealed in His holy Word, our Bible. Whether being employed to steer a ship through a raging sea storm or a believer through the inevitable storms of life, the anchors serve a similar purpose—to bring all safely to harbor.

It is the wise sailor who employs his anchors to keep his vessel afloat. It is the wise believer who employs his Bible to do the same with his faith, especially when it is under attack in hurricane seasons of anxiety, despair, or fear and at risk of sinking. The Bible's prongs of faith are designed to sink deeply into the soul, anchoring it against such seasons. Feel their power to level the rockiness, to steady the trembling, to speak peace:

"In my anguish I cried to the Lord, and he answered me. The Lord is with me; I will not be afraid. What can man do to me? It is better to take refuge in the Lord than to trust in man."

~Psalm 118:5–8

"Do not let your hearts be troubled. Believe in God, believe also in me."

~John 14:1 [NRSV]

"Trust in the Lord with all your heart and lean not to your own understanding. In all your ways, acknowledge him and he will make your paths straight."

~Proverbs 3:5–6

Recall the unwavering faith of Abraham and Moses, Noah, Job and Daniel to name but a few in our biblical history, to punctuate the belief that faith is a ready anchor in stormy times; something that we can hold on to as a support.

The examples of God's faithfulness to us and the faithful witness of our biblical ancestors abound in the Bible. Within its pages we come to understand that faith anchors are typically unseen with the natural eye. To activate their use, several conditions must first be met. There must exist a belief in God's divine sovereignty; that He can do, and does do, things that defy human rationale; that His ways and thoughts are impossible for us to fathom, but we accept them nonetheless. Such acceptance leads to the second condition—the ability to completely trust God; to trust Him even when what He says defies common sense or logic, is without visible, concrete evidence and cannot be proven. And the third condition is the acceptance of God's will for humanity as revealed in His Son, Jesus Christ. These three conditions—belief in God's sovereignty, trust in His ways and thoughts, and acceptance of His will revealed in Jesus—are the cornerstones of active faith.

The dictionary defines faith as a "strong *belief in God or in the doctrines of a religion, based on spiritual apprehension rather than proof.*" How clear it becomes that Jesus is indeed an anchor for our faith when we read His words to the disciples as His earthly ministry drew to its preordained closure.

Jesus had shown Himself to be both a reliable and a principal support to those who accepted Him as God's Son. The fact of His existence as divine and human was and is an anchor of faith. No matter the turmoil of the times, the fear of the unknown, the disappointment of dashed dreams, we need not be troubled. We need only secure our spiritual anchors—belief in God's sovereignty, trust in His ways, and acceptance of His will revealed in Jesus—and like a ship's captain, cast them out, knowing we are ready, our anchors in place to make it safely to harbor.

CHAPTER 7

A THREE-YEAR MINISTRY
That Changed the World

The Son of God/Son of Man was on an urgent mission. He had lived thirty of his preordained thirty-three years, and the clock was ticking. He'd known when He laid aside His divinity for that of a mortal that the allotted time to complete that mission was finite. In fact, He had known from the moment God said, *"Let us make mankind in our image, in our likeness,"* (Genesis 1:26) that this period in the chronicle of the beings they together had created would come. And so, in and around 6 BC, He was born to a teenage girl, who would marry a man named Joseph, in Bethlehem, the city of David. Other than the story of him at age 12 going AWOL for three days, before being located by his parents conversing with the temple elders, we know little of his early childhood. For whatever reasons the scriptures do not allude to that period, nor to his adolescence or early adult years.

Perhaps we can be excused for wondering why Jesus waited to begin His ministry three short years away from His crucifixion; why didn't He begin it sooner? His abilities to engage the temple teachers and amaze them with His questions and answers suggest He was not the average preteen. That episode alone also indicates Jesus did not need a Pauline-like Arabian desert experience to prepare Him for ministry. But three years is not a long time. And for someone on a mission such as His—selecting and preparing a motley group comprised mostly of unschooled Jewish fishermen to execute the The Great Commission—*"Go therefore and make disciples of all nations, baptizing them in the name of the Father and of the Son and of the Holy*

Spirit, and teaching them to obey everything that I have commanded you..." (Matthew 28:19–20) Somehow that time frame seems hardly enough. Yet God's word allays doubt and gives assurance:

> *"Is anything too hard for the Lord?"*
>
> ~Genesis 18:14

> *"For your thoughts are not my thoughts, neither are your ways my ways."*
>
> ~Isaiah 55:8

> *"What is impossible with man is possible with God."*
>
> ~Luke 18:27

The implementation of Jesus' three-year ministry began after His baptism in the Jordan River by His cousin, John the Baptist who had heralded Jesus as the one who *"will baptize with the Holy Spirit."* The Gospel writers chronicle His actions and teachings from that moment to His crucifixion and resurrection three years later. What can we glean from that brief three years of His life in and around what we term today The Holy Land? What were the lessons He taught during such a short time that were so profound that a movement based upon them transformed the world? Because we understand God to be a God of order, not chaos; a God with a plan for all He created, we can assume that Jesus' ministry was neither random nor haphazard; that He had a mental outline for His ministry that we can juxtapose with the primary components of a syllabus: course description, course objectives, and course methodology.

His mission began following His 40-day wilderness experience. As scripture records:

> *"From that time on Jesus began to peach, 'Repent, for the kingdom of heaven has come near.'"*
>
> ~Matthew 4:17

> *"The time has come," He said. "The kingdom of God has come near.*

Repent and believe the good news."

~Mark 1:15

Standing in the synagogue on the Sabbath, He read from the prophet Isaiah, *"The Spirit of the Lord is on me, because he has anointed me to proclaim good news to the poor. He has sent me to proclaim freedom for the prisoners and recovery of sight for the blind, to set the oppressed free, to proclaim the year of the Lord's favor... Today this scripture is fulfilled in your hearing."* (Luke 4:18–19, 21) With these words, Jesus presented the course description of His ministry: He was the "good news" sent in the flesh to redeem mankind and restore its broken relationship with God. Similarly, Jesus' course objectives during those brief three years of itinerant preaching were clear. His teachings would lay the foundations for a religious upheaval which eventually swept across the known world. Those teachings and demonstrations of divinity turned pagan beliefs and traditions upside down, setting the stage for the "people of the way" to become known as Christians, "Christ followers;" and Christianity to be a dominant religious force.

Finally, it is in the methodology of Jesus' syllabus that we come to terms with the brevity of His active ministry. Teaching methodologies typically fall into one of four models:

1. teacher-centered methods
2. learner-centered methods
3. content-centered methods
4. or interactive/participative methods.

Though none of the methods is deemed superior to the others, circumstances and situations tend to dictate which will be more effective. In Jesus' case, with a mission dependent upon time, the first three would not prove fruitful for His purposes. His unschooled fishermen and laborers needed a combination of the first three; and thus, He chose the "interactive/participative" approach. In three years, He lectured in synagogues, preached on seashores, at open air gatherings (precursor to tent meetings?), held "disciples-only" after-hours study sessions, told parables, healed the infirm, demonstrated His power over nature, performed countless miracles, raised the dead, challenged the religious authorities, exposed hypocrisy, and exegeted the Old

Testament in a manner that gave hope to an oppressed people. His fledging band of disciples listened, watched, questioned, mimicked, and finally when He deemed them ready, traveled two by two to themselves proclaim the Good News of Jesus Christ and what He commanded. They weren't perfect; they stumbled, they failed, but they did not give up. Guided and encouraged by the Holy Spirit, they matured sufficiently in those three years such that Jesus could face crucifixion and death, confident that He had accomplished His mission. The cornerstone was laid. The expedited degree program successful. Glory to God, the Master professor for whom nothing is too hard; not even the transformation of a motley crew into followers worthy to be called Jesus' Disciples. And He did it in three years!

CHAPTER 8

In His Shelter and Shadow

"He who dwells in the shelter of the Most High will rest in the shadow of the Almighty."

~Psalm 91:1 NIV

"You who live in the shelter of the Most High, who abide in the shadow of the Almighty…"

~Psalm 91:1 NRSV

For a very long time Psalm 91 has been a staple in my cupboard of scriptures and devotional materials. In the kitchen residing next to my Keurig is a wooden sign that reads *"A day without coffee is like… just kidding. I have no idea!"* I can say the same of Psalm 91—a day without reading it is unimaginable to me. Irrespective of the version in which it is written, the power of the words is addictive. Like my morning cup of java, it is foundational to the start of my day.

Five years ago, this undated and anonymous psalm, possibly collected during the reign of King Hezekiah, took on even greater meaning. Following my only son's stroke and his continuing rehabilitation today from its after effects, I began reading it aloud to him. So often have I read its words for both him and myself, I am sure they are imprinted in the recesses of our minds and hearts. Each reading concludes with the affirmation: *"The word of God for the people of God. Thanks be to God. Amen."*

Why this Psalm? What is its appeal? In this time and these places where we live and move and strive to be faithful in a culture of faithlessness, what does Psalm 91 offer a mother praying for the release of her son from the shackles of a stroke and his reemergence on to a recovery path that will lead him to a renewed life? What does it offer a son who listens to the familiar voice of his mother reading these words over and over again? How do they or anyone of us dwell in God's shelter and rest in His shadow; especially during times of trial that seem unending?

From a limited human perspective, the word "shelter" is relatively common. In its simplest terms, it's a place, a lodging of some sort—a house or an apartment; even an outdoor dwelling like a cave or a tent qualifies as a shelter. At the non-tangible level, a shelter often refers to a sanctuary, a haven, something that offers security, a protector. When natural disasters threaten, we seek protection in secure places designed to prevent damage or harm; when manmade disasters loom, we depend upon authorities to defend and shield us. Psalm 91 however compels us to look beyond the commonplace understanding of "shelter." It pushes us to the concept of a precursor to the sheltering: *"He who dwells in…"* The onus to avail ourselves of God's shelter is upon us. His shelter is stationary; it remains in place awaiting our decision to seek it as our place of refugee; our sanctuary, our haven. Ours is the decision to make. Do we satisfy ourselves with shelters of our own design and make—our possessions, our accomplishments, our wealth, our status? Are these "shelters" sufficient to protect and provide for us when dangers drop and stop the progression of our lives? The wise among us—and hopefully you, dear reader, fall into that category—know the answer is a resounding "NO."

The shelter of God is found in His Presence, His Word, and the indwelling of His Holy Spirit. *"In the shelter of your presence you hide them…"* David declares of God in Psalm 31:20. *"Let the word of God dwell in you richly,"* Paul writes to the believers in Colossae. *"Likewise, the Spirit helps us in our weakness; for we do not know how to pray as we ought, but that very Spirit intercedes.…And God who searches the heart, knows what is the mind of the Spirit.…,"* Paul explains in Romans 8:26–27. Not even the most sophisticated manmade shelter existing today can compare to the shelter God provides. No weapon can touch those enveloped by His omnipresence. No earthly opinions, arguments, or data can refute His everlasting words. Nothing can thwart the moving of His Holy Spirit as He so wills.

When these three elements of dwelling in His shelter are in place, we find our rest in the shadow provided. Commonly, a shadow is thought of as a dark area produced when something comes between light and a surface. It also describes something gloomy or ominous; or is used to reference something insubstantial or fleeting. The *shadow of the Almighty*" falls into none of these categories. To the contrary, the shadow cast by God is a barrier and a refuge. It serves as a haven for the weary during trying times. It blocks sadness and fear. And perhaps most importantly, the shadow of the Almighty is sturdy and sound; neither transient nor cursory, but lasting and eternal. It allows us to proclaim, *"I will say of the Lord, He is my refuge and my fortress."* (Psalm 91:2) His shelter and His shadow are His promises that enable us to hold on; to not despair; to wait in faith for the manifestation of His words:

> *"Because he loves me,'" says the Lord, "I will rescue him; I will protect him, for he acknowledges my name. He will call upon me, and I will answer him; I will be with him in trouble, I will deliver him and honor him. With long life I will I satisfy him and show him my salvation.'"*
>
> ~Psalm 91:14–16

Rest in the moment in order to live in the moments to be is the reward of the promises of Psalm 91. That is why I read it and why my son listens. It is our refuge during this season.

CHAPTER 9

A HILLSIDE PICNIC

*"Then Jesus directed them to have all the people sit down in groups
on the green grass. So they sat down in groups of hundreds and fifties."*
~Mark 6:39–40

*"But he said to his disciples, 'Have them sit down in groups of
about fifty each.' The disciples did so, and everybody sat down."*
~Luke 14:15

*"Jesus said, 'Have the people sit down.' There was plenty of grass
in that place, and the men sat down, about five thousand of them."*
~John 6:10

Picnics easily bring to mind the local park or grassy field shaded
by large trees where families and/or friends gather, relaxing on
blankets or beach chairs; coolers nearby as they share potluck
dishes and grilled burgers and hot dogs. Recently, something I
was reading described the familiar account of Jesus feeding the
5,000 as a sort of "picnic." I don't recall the full gist of the piece;
nonetheless the descriptor stuck, and here we are—looking at
this Jesus-miracle through 21st century lens; in the hope that a
whimsical twist affirms still that who Jesus was then is who He is
now—a miracle worker.

Perhaps the first aspect of the miracle that He foreknew He
would be performing that day is the location in which it occurred.
It was as Matthew writes, *"a solitary place,"* one to which Jesus had
withdrawn in hopes that He and the disciples might as Mark pens,

"get some rest." And though the area was surrounded by villages, it was remote enough that it would have been impossible for those first century markets to meet the sustenance needs of the 5,000 men and uncounted women and children. Thus, the stage was set by the site itself for a miracle to occur. The hillside (as we assume it to have been) was a grassy area. Not unlike areas today where folks gather for a picnic. As the day wore on in that remote spot, only something miraculous could address the people's eventual need for food, as apparently taking provisions with you as you followed Jesus from place to place was not common practice. One can imagine Jesus, gazing over the multitude, perhaps thinking what a perfect opportunity to address both the physical and spiritual needs of these for whom He felt such compassion. So, in that green, grassy park-like setting, the "picnic" was set in motion.

The practical disciples suggested that Jesus send the people away to buy food. His response, *"No, you give them something to eat,"* no doubt boggled their minds. All four gospel writers reference the mass feeding story lending credence to its veracity. Only the Apostle John's version though has a boy as the source of the fish and bread:

> *"Here is a boy with five small barley loaves and two small fish, but how will they go among so many?"*
>
> ~John 6:9

That Jesus expected the disciples to supply the food is implied by Luke who writes,

> *He replied, "You give them something to eat."*
>
> ~Luke 9:13

Perhaps the picnic analogy gets its impetus at this point in the story. The thousands of people seated in varying groups, reclining on the grass seemed amazingly peaceful, as folks tend to be at a picnic gathering. As Jesus took the meager fish and bread, blessed it and gave it to the disciples to disburse, the "picnickers" simply waited their turn to receive a serving; just as one might at a typical picnic today. No need to rush the serving tables or the various picnic baskets or crowd the guys at the grill. There's always enough food at a picnic. It wasn't any different then as Jesus, the host, provided more than enough, and everyone had their fill.

I propose that only a handful of folk other than the disciples initially perceived what happened that day. Probably just the people in closest proximity to Jesus as He blessed two fish and five loaves began to marvel and whisper as the filled baskets passed amongst them. They and the disciples would be eyewitnesses to this miracle—the multiplication of two fish and five loaves of bread into enough food for everyone, with 12 baskets of leftovers. In a tranquil setting on a grassy hillside, Jesus' words filled their spiritual hunger and His multiplication miracle satisfied their physical needs.

His dual nourishment has not ceased. The words He spoke to the crowd that day were not lost to antiquity. The Bible, still the best-selling and most translated book in human history, contains those very words, the teachings that resounded over the quiet murmurings of that first century crowd. On an even grander scale, His feeding of the 5,000 plus continues. In places across this nation and throughout the world, hungry people are fed through the efforts of individuals, churches, and other entities. The fact that they labor in this "feeding of the hungry" work speaks in my mind to the miracle of Jesus' presence today; looking with compassion and prompting us: *"You give them something to eat."* In contemporary times when many share the initial reaction of the disciples: "Send them away to get some food to eat; we have nothing to give them," Jesus' spirit prompts the opposite. That prompting is an expression of His continuing miracles. His compassion matched by action met the physical needs of the multitude. His teachings in the 25th chapter of Matthew instruct us to do the same. When we encounter hungry people, we are moved to feed them. As He did at the "picnic," we are to provide what others need when they are without. When we do that, a miracle occurs. Jesus' divinity manifests itself in our obedience; His image in our actions.

CHAPTER 10

GOD'S WAITING SEASONS

"Wait for the Lord; be strong and take heart and wait for the Lord."
                                                          ~Psalm 27:13–14

In 1789, Benjamin Franklin word the familiar phrase "...*in this world, nothing is certain except death and taxes,*" in a letter. According to *The Yale Book of Quotations*, however, a certain Christopher Bullock used similar wording in 1716—"*Tis impossible to be sure of anything but Death and Taxes,*" and Edward Ward wrote, "*Death and Taxes, they are certain,*" in 1724. Regardless of its origin, the phrase is commonly recognized as an apt description of two of life's sureties: death and taxes. If you're human, you'll not escape either. Exercising literary license, I'd like to expand the phrase as follows: "*Nothing in the world is certain except death, taxes, and waiting seasons.*"

"Umm," you say, "I get death and taxes; but waiting seasons?"

Yes, gentle reader, the phenomenon of waiting seasons is as much a reality as the finality of death and the assessment of taxes. Seasons of waiting complete the trilogy of "life—certainty" experiences. Irrespective of gender, age, ethnicity, financial or social status, at some appointed time, *Death* will tap your shoulder, *IRS* will send the tax assessment, and the *Waiting Season* bell will toll. Whether the waiting occurs at a doctor's office, in designated places in the ICU at the hospital, in the principal's office, outside the boss' inner sanctum, in chairs at the unemployment hub, in the space abutting the counselor's cubicle, in the lobby at the DMV, at home alone after the loss of a loved one, in the living room as the clock ticks past the teenager's curfew, next to the bedside of an aged parent in the nursing home, in the courtroom—a waiting season's appointed time will come. Because God both allows and orchestrates these times according to His plans and purposes, they are a metaphor of His words. As He speaks in Isaiah 55, *"As the heavens are higher than the earth, so are my ways higher than your ways and my thoughts than your thoughts. As the rain and the snow come down from heaven, and do not return to it without watering the earth and making it bud and flourish so that it yields seed for the sower and bread for the eater, so is my word that goes out from my mouth; it will not return to me empty, but will accomplish what I desire and achieve the purpose for which I sent it."*

Waiting seasons serve God's purposes, and the time we spend in them can sharpen and deepen our relationship with Him, if we allow them to. As the word He speaks does not return void, neither does His waiting season. It produces His image in believers who master the time they spend there.

Believers are a waiting people. Waiting is the premise upon which our faith is built. Sprinkled throughout the biblical landscape of our sacred word are verses that speak to waiting. Walk with me now through some of these passages:

In the morning, O Lord, you hear my voice; in the morning I lay my requests before you and wait in expectation.
~Psalm 5:3

Wait for the Lord; be strong and take heart and wait for the Lord.
~Psalm 27:14

We wait in hope for the Lord; he is our hope and our shield.
~Psalm 33:20

Wait for the Lord and keep His way.
~Psalm 37:34

Be still before the Lord and wait patiently for him…
~Psalm 37:7

I wait for you, O Lord; you will answer, O Lord, my God.

~Psalm 38:15

I waited patiently for the Lord; he turned to me and heard my cry. He lifted me out of the slimy pit, out of the mud and mire; he set my feet on a rock and gave me a firm place to stand.

~Psalm 40:1–2

I wait for the Lod, my soul waits, and in his word, I put my hope. My soul waits for the Lord more than watchmen wait for the morning.

~Psalm 130:5–6

It is good to wait quietly for the salvation of the Lord.

~Lamentations 3:26

…but those who wait for the Lord shall renew their strength, they shall mount up with wings like eagles, they shall run and not be weary, they shall walk and not faint.

~Isaiah 40:31

For the Lord is a God of justice; blessed are all those who wait for him.

~Isaiah 30:18

Lord, be gracious to us; we wait for you.

~Isaiah 33:2

But as for me, I will look to the Lord, I will wait for the God of my salvation; my God will hear me.

~Micah 7:7

But if we hope for what we do not see, we wait for it with patience.

~Romans 8:25

For through the spirit by, faith, we eagerly wait for the hope of righteousness.

~Galatians 5:5

And so after waiting patiently, Abraham received what was promised.

~Hebrews 6:15

Like death that has its appointed time and taxes its deadlines, waiting seasons too have a time fame; and despite the emotional turmoil they may cause during those periods—impatience, irritation, anxiety, anger, fear, resignation, helplessness, and despair, they are finite. As the afore referenced scriptures suggest, times of waiting are testing times. They can as the saying goes, "make us or break us." We can choose to use them as building blocks of faith. Their very inevitability affords opportunities to trust God more; to believe that our waiting is within the unseen chapters that He writes of our story. By His grace these seasons of waiting can and should strengthen our relationship with Him as we grow in patience and trust and hope. So, as you come of age, pay your taxes; resign yourself to the surety of death's calling card and sandwich between the two the building of your spiritual self. Allow these waiting seasons to fulfill the purposes for which God permits them—you becoming more like Jesus.

CHAPTER 11

"Vicki's Gone"

"... for death is the destiny of every man; the living should take this to heart."

~Ecclesiastes 7:2

I admit my wonder as I set out to write this reflection. It features death, one of the members of the Three Life Certainties referenced in the preceding one. Such a sequence was not planned. But as I trust God to both inspire and direct my word crafting, I will assume it is as it is intended to be. To many of us the natural aura that hovers over a nursing home is one of finality. It's a place where we are not surprised when a resident makes the transition from life to death. But if you have had—as I have—a reason to visit such a facility on a regular basis, over time the expectancy of this life certainty fades; you forget about it. Instead, you come to know the residents and anticipate them being in place each time you walk through the doors. Such was my expectation a couple of years ago on that fateful day which prompts this piece.

Vicki was annoying; the kind of person who, as old folks would say, had to "grow on ya." She appeared to be somewhere in her sixties, perhaps older; but often as it is with people who are "kissed by the sun" at birth, hard to say. Asking would have been impolite and not really my business anyway. You could hear her loud, brash voice as soon as you started down the corridor to the resident rooms. The pre-pandemic protocols encouraged resident gatherings in the both the TV and dining rooms. It was also common for them to traverse the hallways in their wheelchairs if they were able. So, if you didn't meet Vicki propelling herself along the corridor to the lobby area, you could pinpoint her presence in one of the gathering spaces by the sound of her voice. She was a talker, offering unsolicited commentary during Bible study as the facilitator waited patiently for her to be quiet so he could continue his point; talking continuingly and loudly to the television characters as if she were in the show. Perhaps her loquaciousness was a manifestation of a particular health condition; or maybe that was just her personality. But whatever the reason, her behavior was annoying—to me anyway. And in my mind reason enough to confine her to her room. But the staff never did that; and the other residents seldom asked her to "shut up."

As I stated at the onset, Vicki grew on you. As the years passed and my son continued his sojourn in the Lord's workshop there at the nursing home, Vicki's spontaneous talkativeness lost its sting. When I exercised the patience I was always praying to possess, her comments ceased to be annoying; more often they were funny or surprisingly insightful. Vicki was Vicki; and you accepted her as she was, realizing she was not mean-spirited. She made me think of what a special needs child might grow up to be—without society's common filters—still expressive and open to life's promises. In fact, she was genuine in her concern for her co-residents. Hers was the spirit in the room that uplifted the others. Vicki made them smile; and soon enough she had me doing the same. A visit without running into her just wasn't the same.

As I made my way to the residential area of the nursing home that day, I sensed an unfamiliar quietness, a hush almost. Few were in either the social room or dining area. When I got to the nurse's station before entering my son's room, I asked a passing staff member why everyone seemed so somber.

She paused. "*Vicki's gone,*" she whispered softly.

"*Gone where?*" I responded, thinking she meant Vicki had been transported for some emergency to the hospital—a common enough scenario I'd witnessed on any number of occasions.

"*No, she died. During the night. When they went in this morning to get her up, she was gone.*"

My heart flipped. I couldn't process what she'd said. I sputtered, "*But I just saw her two days ago. She was fine. How can she be dead?*"

In retrospect I realize that was the dumbest question a professed follower of Jesus Christ could have allowed to spill from her lips. Despite my "saved and sanctified" status, my initial reaction to the Grim Reaper who is never satisfied was no different than that of a pagan or non-believer. "How can she be dead?" Easily enough as we all know. Death doesn't seek permission. *"There is a time for everything,"* scripture tells us—*"a time to be born and a time to die."* (Ecclesiastes 3:20) I know and believe this truth, and still I acted contrary to my belief. Why? I suspect because like all of us on this journey to eternity, we're works in progress until either we ourselves shed this mortal cloak or Jesus returns as promised. We know the truth, but that knowledge has not yet freed us from failure. God's grace alone does that. His grace provides correction, forgives us, sets us back on the path, frees us to try again and again to get it right. I could not take back the words I spoke as my initial reaction to Vicki's demise. I was stunned by her sudden passing, but I ought to have recovered more quickly and offered words of comfort instead of astonishment. It has taken me a while to come to terms with this slip. But it has also made me more aware of how our faith is revealed most in what we say and do, especially in times of crisis or pain.

CHAPTER 12

THE SMG THREESOME

Sin: Crime, trespass, wrongdoing, immorality, iniquity, blasphemy, evil, misdeed, sacrilege, transgression against divine law.

Mercy: Forgiveness shown toward someone whom it is within one's power to punish, leniency, clemency, forbearance, charity.

Grace: Within the Christian faith, the belief in the free and unmerited favor of God as shown in the salvation offered mankind via the crucifixion of Jesus Christ, compassion.

Why this threesome continues its streak of being the longest running show of all times can be puzzling. When the first of the Threesome, Sin, took to the stage over 6,000 years ago, no one would have predicted its recording-breaking run; its influence, its stamp upon humankind. There in the setting of a beautiful garden filled with all they needed to live abundantly and sin-free, our biblical ancestors, swayed by Sin's deceptiveness, turned up their noses to their Creator, Writer and Director; and they chose to listen to the seductive voice of a stagehand. With their disobedience, act one of the chronicles of mankind became one not of glory, but shame, punishment, and banishment. Sin had moved from a possibility to a surety in the annuals of human history. As scripture so tells, in a short time it cemented its existence in the human narrative.

> "Then the Lord said to Cain, 'Why are you angry? Why is your face downcast? If you do what is right, will you not be accepted? But if you do not do what is right, sin is crouching at your door; it desires to have you, but you must master it.'"
>
> ~Genesis 4:6–7

From the human perspective, 6,000 years is a long time. It is from that perspective that I write this exegesis simply in the hope of encouraging someone to not despair in a world where it's easy to do so as the *clock keeps on ticking* and sin keeps on *tricking*. Sin is ubiquitous. It touches every aspect of life. It is no respecter of age, gender, ethnicity, economic status, educational level, professional attainment, job description, whether you reside in a mansion or a hovel on the street. Sin is pervasive. Following that little *tete-a-tete* in the garden, the curtain was thrown open to its guile, its evil, its immorality.

What might have appeared as Sin's complete victory was soon squashed, however. Before Sin could slither away, the Creator, Writer, and Director commenced with act two of the drama. The second of the Threesome, Mercy, moved gracefully onto center stage. The Creator's words of punishment for our ancestors' sin were harsh. And although they should have died, He chose instead to extend mercy, both by sparing their lives and providing for their physical wellbeing.

> *"The Lord God made garments of skin for Adam and his wife and clothed them."*
>
> ~Genesis 3:21

His extension of mercy and forgiveness began the see-saw saga of mankind's disobedience and his subsequent pleas for leniency. In the 4,000 plus years to follow, Sin and Mercy would dominate the biblical scene. Time after time, men would transgress God's laws and commandments. His punishments would follow until the people would plead for forgiveness and swear to turn from their sins. And He would revise the script once again; turn from His anger and wrath and shower them with unmerited blessings; mercy poured out in spite of their disobedience.

At the heart of the Old Testament writings are these *yin and yang* performances of Sin and Mercy. But the curtain closed on them around 430 BC with the writings of the prophet Malachi, and 400 years would pass before the birth of Jesus between 6–4 BC, and the written accounts of His life and its subsequent impact as recorded in the New Testament ushered in a revival of this divine stage production.

The seemingly unending cycle of the interplay between Sin and Mercy had defined the relationship of God and humankind. And despite the revolving door through which they moved; the people still believed God would one day bring peace to the land promised to their ancestors. They continued to wait for the promised Messiah who they believed would bring that about. But something drastic was needed to break the *one step forward, two steps backwards* rhythm of their lives; something that had could break that cycle and restore their relationship with God.

With the birth of Jesus, the Writer and Director knew the time had come for the third of the Threesome to make its appearance on humanity's stage. The third entity, Grace, in the persona of Jesus, the Christ, completed the trio. With Jesus in form both human and divine, the Director was ready for the final revision of His script. God knew His creation. Because of sin's hold they would always stray; they would repent, and He would be merciful in the moment as they did so. But under the law they would still be held solely accountable for their sins. The Grace of the Threesome was not the grace spoken of in the Old Testament. This was ultimate grace offered freely to those who had done nothing to receive it; grace shown in the salvation offered to humanity by Jesus' crucifixion, death and resurrection. As the Apostle Paul writes in 2 Corinthians 5:21, *"God made him who had no sin to be sin for us, so in him we might become the righteousness of God."* The grace personified in Jesus would open the door to the restoration of humanity to its Creator. Mercy had been a temporary solution; it soothed the discord for only so long. Grace made eternity a possibility for even the worse sinner. When confession of sin was joined by an acceptance of and belief in Jesus' divinity and resurrection, the hold of sin was broken; the restoration of the Creator to His creation was realized. Yes, sin still exists, and God's mercy is ever present, but thank God, Grace took its place alongside them. For when the inevitability of sin damages our relationship with the Divine and the patch of His Mercy isn't enough to repair it, Grace alone provides a way back to Him. Unfailing grace; the key that opens the door to eternity.

CHAPTER 13

Who's to Blame?

"The man said, 'The woman whom you gave to be with me, she gave me fruit from the tree, and I ate it.' Then the Lord God said to the woman, 'What is this you have done?' The woman said, 'The serpent tricked me and I ate.'"

~Genesis: 3:12–13

Blame or blaming others specifically, seems easily to have slipped into the human DNA and thus into the lexicon not long after our origin. As the exchange between God and the man and woman reveal, the first recorded responses of our biblical ancestors were words of blame; pointing the proverbial finger at a third party, a serpent mind you, for their having done something wrong. In an article entitled, "*Why We Blame Others*, Ana Gonzalez defines the act of blaming as "assigning responsibility for a fault or wrong." She adds, "the reason why people usually blame others is that it's a quick escape from guilt," and it gives the blamers a sense that they bear no responsibility for what happened.

On August 31, 2021, the longest war in this country's history ended as the last member of our military forces boarded the plane headed back to the US. For 20 years Americans in the military and private sectors fought to eradicate terrorism and to help build a nation in a country unable to achieve those goals unaided by others. Their efforts failed. Four American presidents wrestled with this issue, as have the American people. The evacuations of military personnel and Afghanistan people who worked for them during the years of occupation were chaotic, mirroring images of this nation's withdrawal following the Vietnam war. These recent images colored by cable news media and unending commentary of politicians of all persuasions bring me to the point of this reflection, the ascendancy of blame to an unwarranted position in the national discourse. Blaming the current president for choosing to adhere to the date set by his immediate predecessor for the final withdrawal of our troops bears the earmarks of the essence of blaming. The name of the game today is Blame. After all is said and done, the tendency to place blame is shaping the moment.

Newspaper headlines and editorials, cable anchors and their experts, Democrats, Republicans, legislators of all stripes are finger pointers. Laying the blame at the president's door assuages individual and collective guilt. Focusing attention upon the concluding act of an effort (perhaps doomed from its inception) distorts the reality of collective responsibility for all that preceded it. And as we are witnessing, it allows blame to be placed elsewhere.

These times that surely *try men's (and women's) souls* are ripe for all who profess Jesus as their Savior to turn to His words when the temptation to blame takes hold.

> *"Do not judge, so that you may not be judged. For with the judgment, you make you will be judged, and the measure you give will be the measure you get. Why do you see the speck in your neighbor's eye, but do not notice the log in your own eye? Or how can you say to your neighbor, 'Let me take the speck out of your eye, while the log is still in your own eye? You hypocrite, first take the log out of your own eye, and then you will see clearly to take the speck out of your neighbor's eye."*
>
> ~Matthew 7:1–5 [NRSV]

The metaphor is clear. Before pointing the finger at our current president and blaming him for the actions he took to bring a long overdue conflict to its end, those who helped fuel it during the past 20 years need to look inward; a reality check for their roles and their acceptance of what was wrong. Casting the blame alone at the president's feet is akin to seeing his faults and refusing to acknowledge your own. Self-examination rather than blaming is called for. No one person is responsible for the conflict, nor for its aftermath. None of us can judge whether or not the conclusion of this chapter in the annals of America's involvement in nation-building could have been avoided. We weren't in the room. Individually and collectively, we the people of the United States who profess to know Jesus (and that's the vast majority of us) are called to a higher standard. With faults of our own to reconcile, we turn from playing the blame game. We show compassion. We embrace the teachings of our faith and seek the good, even in the midst of the bad. No one individual is to blame for the outcome we've witnessed. We all have played a part, willingly or unwillingly, in this saga of human history. We are all to blame.

"Therefore, you have no excuse, whoever you are, when you judge others, for in passing judgment upon another you condemn yourself, because you the judge, are doing the very same things."
~Romans 2:1 [NRSV]

CHAPTER 14

Prolonged Adolescence

"When I was a child, I talked like a child, I thought like a child, I reasoned like a child. When I became a man(woman), I put childish ways behind me."

~1 Corinthians 13:11

The word, *adolescence*, entered the lexicon in the 15th century; its origins traced to the Latin word, *adolescere*, meaning *to grow up or to grow into maturity*. But it wasn't until the early 1900s that the term came into use in the western world when the president of the American Psychological Association, G. Stanley Hall, used it in a study entitled, "Adolescence." He employed the term to describe the developmental stage caused by social changes in the 20th century that affected children. With the advent of Child Labor Laws and universal education, the responsibilities of adulthood were no longer forced upon them. The years from 13 to approximately 21 became free of adult burdens and pursuits. Instead, a culture developed that reshaped those years into a time in which individuals of that age group were *defining* themselves; growing less dependent upon parents, and forming closer relationships with people outside their family circle. (Credit: Boston Youth Arts Evaluation Project, as recounted by the Mass Cultural Council 2021) You need not be a parent to know that we live in an era when the stages of human development are blurry. Well beyond the adolescent years, many individuals linger in dependence upon aging parents; or demonstrate off-and-on patterns of dependency and independence. They seem unable to move beyond the elementary stages of maturity into commonly accepted adult behaviors.

While the discourse surrounding the developmental stages of growth and maturity has varying perspectives, the Bible's singular reference to human maturity seems clear. As the scripture above notes, how children speak, think and reason is not the same as how adults do. And when one reaches maturity, i.e., adulthood, one is expected to shed the trappings of childhood. I posit we can say the same of our spiritual growth and maturity.

In the initial stages of faith, we mimic the enthusiasm of adolescents who've just turned 13. As they embrace the moniker *teenager*, we hail our identity as *Christians*. But all too often our spiritual growth imitates some of the negativisms that define the adolescence stage. We need not necessarily have parented an adolescent to know what these behaviors are; having passed through this stage ourselves, we can own some of them: lying, arguing, defiance, awkwardness, abandoning commitments, withdrawal, attitude, impulsiveness being some of the most common. And though we may have shed these behaviors in the physical and emotional, often we cannot say the same in the realm of our spirituality. Perhaps now is a good time to do a self-assessment of the state of your spiritual maturity. Your reflections upon the behaviors that follow hopefully give you pause; and prompt you to ask yourself if you have "put childish ways behind you" or if you remain a believer caught in the trap of extended adolescence.

- Are you continually confessing the same sins over and over? Offering excuses for why?
- Do you try to hide your faults from fellow believers hoping to avoid their judgment or the withdrawal of their love or friendship?
- Are you easily led to argue, defending your position or perspective at all costs?
- Do you disdain correction?
- Do you defy Christian norms without seeking God's guidance from His word or prayer?
- Do you tend to be extremely self-critical or feel unworthy of God's love and redemption?

- Do you, when reading or hearing the foundational truths of God's word, take exception and dismiss it as irrelevant to your life?
- Are you known to have an *attitude* about most things, such that others step lightly in your presence to avoid your display of temper?
- Are you a willing, spontaneous giver? Or quite content to always be on the receiving end?
- Does impulsivity describe your approach to life, often acting first and thinking later?
- Do you struggle to keep commitments, or is it easy to chalk things up with an "I forgot?"
- Do you continue to stay close to the Savior you've confessed as Lord of your life by living daily to please and honor Him? Or is this something you think is not all that important?
- What do you think God would say about the level of your spiritual maturity at this season of your life?

No one is perfect. We all sin and come short of God's glory and His purposes for our lives. In truth we are incapable of any maturity on our own. We need the indwelling of the Holy Spirit daily to help us grow in it. As we surrender to its leading, we realize we grow in faith maturation by being obedient to God's teachings revealed in His holy Word. And as we mature in faith, throwing off childishness and adolescent trappings, we move closer to our ultimate goal of hearing the Lord proclaim, "Well done, good and faithful servant!"

CHAPTER 15:

INSECT WORRIES

"Do not be anxious about anything, but in everything, by prayer and petition, with thanksgiving, present your requests to God. And the peace of God which transcends all understanding, will guard your hearts and your minds in Christ Jesus."

~Philippians 4:6–7

At first glance the title seems an oxymoron. How can the situations that cause worry be compared to an insect? Afterall, insects are little creatures that aren't all that important in the greater scheme of life. Surely human worries have nothing in common with them. Oh, contraire, dear reader. Just as a small bug of one kind or another—a wood-eating termite, a cloth-eating moth, a plant-nibbling aphid—has the ability to wreak havoc and cause agitation and destruction, so do those worries we might term little or insect size. Though on first thought they seem minor, their consistent nibbling has the ability to erode our trust fiber; much like tiny termites contribute to the collapse of wooden buildings and the almost invisible moth leaves holes in garments.

The immediate problem with insect worries is their ability to hold one hostage to life's minutiae. Constant immersion in and preoccupation with the small stuff of living wears down spiritual strength. Common are the laments, "Oh, I know I shouldn't worry, be anxious, feel so uneasy, get so nervous, let the stress get to me, but…" Those universal declarations are beyond count. They are the sound of insect worries having their way and taking their toll. And the long-term effect of bowing to them is discovering that when life's major stuff blows our way, tossing us around like tree leaves, our safety net is gone. We have no reservoir from which to draw. The little worries have so accumulated that we are easy prey for the big ones.

A life surety is that trials and tribulations we count as major do come. Financial issues, wayward children, aging parents, personal health challenges, professional disappointments, natural disasters, manmade catastrophes, death's tap, and a host of other things beyond our control reveal what our lives are built upon. How deeply have we dug the hole in which we planted our spiritual essence? Did we make it wide and deep enough for our faith to grow so that it sustains us during both the minor and major challenges of living? When we read Philippians 4:6-7, *"Do not be anxious about anything, but in everything, by prayer and petition, with thanksgiving, present your requests to God. And the peace of God which transcends all understanding, will guard your hearts and your minds in Christ Jesus."*—are we guilty of not doing what it says? The words are clear. There is nothing about which we are to be anxious or worried. Every time we say we are worried about anything—whether it's our children, grandchildren, other family members, our health, the visit to the doctor, the economy, who's elected to office, the latest weather predictions, crime, racial discord, injustice, fraud, drugs, human trafficking—we disobey the command of this scripture. Nothing during our life's journey should worry us when we have accepted Jesus as God's son and our Savior, by whom we've been redeemed. The antidote to worries—insect or otherwise—is clear. Once we pray and petition with thanksgiving, the worry should cease. If it continues, we have a faith problem. Our spiritual growth is stymied and needs revival. May we look to God's Word to widen and deepen our faith.

"So do not fear, for I am with you; do not be dismayed, for I am your God. I will strengthen you and help you; I will uphold you with my righteous right hand."
~Isaiah 41:10

"Therefore, I tell you, do not worry about your life, what you will

eat or drink; or about your body, what you will wear. Is not life more than food, and the body more than clothes?"

~Matthew 6:25

"Cast all your anxieties on him because he cares for you."

~1 Peter 5:7

"Therefore, do not worry about tomorrow, for tomorrow will worry about itself. Each day has enough trouble of its own."

~Matthew 6:34

When anxiety was great within me, your consolation brought me joy."

~Psalm 94:19

"Do not let your hearts be troubled. Trust in God; trust also in me."

~John 14:1

CHAPTER 16

"Sold Out"

"Shadrach, Meshach and Abednego replied to the king, ... we do not need to defend ourselves before you in this matter. If we are thrown into the blazing furnace, the God we serve is able to save us from it, and he will rescue us from your hand, O king. But even if he does not, we want you to know, O king, that we will not serve your gods or worship the image of gold you have set up."
~Daniel 3:16-18

The story of the three young men who were among the captives during Israel's 70-year exile in Babylon usually focuses upon their show of courage when faced with dire consequences for disobeying the king's edict. True enough, few facing the penalty of being burned alive would display such grit. I postulate their resolve was evidence not just of their bravery, but as importantly, of their faith. If their faith in their God had been shaky or shallow, so too would have been their response to the adversity they faced. After all, until that incident occurred, they had enjoyed the king's favor. By fortune of their birth, education, and social standing, he had elevated them to enter his service; and eventually appointed them administrators over the provinces of Babylon. To forfeit the perks that attended being in the royal inner circle would not have been an easy decision to make. But they made it, and by so doing, take their place among our first testament biblical ancestors as exemplars of the contemporary urban phrase, *sold out*, a phrase used to reference someone who is *"completely committed, devoted, invested and engaged in a cause; to have no reserves about the decision you are making. To be willing to go anywhere, to do anything and give up everything in order to achieve your goal.*" (Urban Dictionary)

As the ancient world evolved and the chronicles of the second testament were written, others too can be identified as being *sold out* for their faith. We can easily proclaim that in the lives of the Apostle Paul and the early Christian martyrs. In their total commitment and devotion to God, they had no hesitation or doubt about their decision; and they were determined to achieve their goal of obedience to His commandments. They were sold-out believers.

In the present age the question is a simple one. Does the moniker hold true for us who profess Christ today? Do our actions bear witness that we are 21st century sold-out believers? What distinguishes us from non-believers as a result of our decision to accept Jesus as God's Son descended from heaven to be born of a virgin; who lived 30-plus years before being crucified and dying; and who on the third day arose from His tomb; and not long thereafter ascended into heaven from which He had come? Do we bow to the pressures of 21st century culture and values that contradict this faith statement? Sadly, for too many of us the answer is, "Yes." Unlike the aforementioned Israelite captives who demonstrated a singled-minded faith, we lean toward double-mindedness in ours. We wear the faith mantle easily when life glides smoothly, contentment filling our days. With ease we speak and sing of the *joy of the Lord*. But oh, how easily that mantle slips from sanctified shoulders, and joy morphs into anxiety, worry, fear when darkness falls; spewing illness, unemployment, death, natural and manmade disasters, children gone astray, broken relationships, depression, or any of the myriad faith testers common to the human experience.

Today, Shadrach, Meshach and Abednego's bold declaration of their faith would likely make the news, with cable anchors and experts, perhaps even religious spokespersons, weighing in; some declaring the fool-heartedness of their actions and others questioning their mental state. Perhaps one or two lone expert believers would seek to explain their actions as appropriate expressions of their faith. But few of us will argue that the tenor of our times does not lend itself to that kind of faith expression. It's too extreme for contemporary culture—social media platforms alone yield such influence that a faith stance like they exhibited could destroy one's standing personally and professionally. Is the kind of risk they took worth taking? Can we continue to say, "Yes, Lord, I'm sold out for You," in one breath and invalidate that vow when any of the afore-mentioned faith testers appear? What can fill our courage tank with fuel to meet testing times with singleminded faith? As pastors are prone to say, "I'm glad you asked!"

God's promises are the best source for the courage needed to exhibit sold-out faith. Shadrach, Meshach and Abednego held to their belief that the God they worshipped was able to protect and rescue them from the trial which they faced. The trial itself had no affect upon that faith; even if God chose not to save them, they would not abandon their faith in Him. Their circumstances did not alter their belief. We worship the same God. He has not changed. Life challenges will occur; situations that test our faith profession will continue. Perhaps the three captives recited the ancient Torah to remind themselves of God's promises as they waited. We are wise to mimic them even when conventional wisdom suggests otherwise. No matter the darkness of the hour, the dangers, the threats to life itself, as believers we are committed to Christ; to His commandments, to His teachings. We wear the badge of His persona irrespective of circumstances. We resist worry, anxiety, fretfulness, fear, despair through immersion in His word. For courage is there; wisdom is there; faithfulness is there. Everything needed to live our faith can be found in His word. Our obedience to it will ensure His, "Well done, good and faithful servant." After all, is that not the goal of sold-out-for-God faith?

CHAPTER 17

SOIL FOR SPIRITUAL GROWTH

"Some fell into good soil, and when it grew, it produced a hundredfold."

~Luke 8:8 [NRSV]

During this past Advent season, I planted an amaryllis bulb as a practicum exercise. It was one of several suggestions put forth in the devotional study guide. It was my first such experience, and I was excited when it arrived, complete with an instructional booklet, soil, and a container in which it was to grow. The soil was rich looking and needed only two more ingredients to ensure the bulb's steady growth over the coming year. With adequate watering and proper sunlight, the instructions advised, by this time next year I would enjoy the beauty of a fully grown plant and know the joy of having played a role in its maturity.

The experience, which as I write is ongoing, prompted me to compare how similar the amaryllis' journey from a misshapen bulb to a brilliant red flowering plant is to that of those who claim the name, "Christian." When first we come to Christ, we are misshapen by sin, unsightly, and not at all pleasing to the Savior; and more than likely even to ourselves. But in that moment when we arrive at His altar whether it's in the sanctuary, the bedroom, the car, the prison cell, the schoolyard, the alley behind the bar, or the hospital bed, and confess our sins and acknowledge Him as the son of God and our personal Savior, we begin the transformation from misshapen to wholeness. Like the amaryllis whose small green shoots begin to emerge from the soil in which it rests, we too begin to reflect an image unlike the one with which we began the journey. As we find our rest in the Savior, we sprout more of His image as the days multiply.

Assuring the growth of my amaryllis requires me to provide it with the proper support. Daily I check its moisture level—is it receiving sufficient water? Periodically I change its position to ensure it's getting the right amount of sunlight. Its growth depends upon these three conditions: the right soil, the right amount of water, and the correct amount of sunshine. If I hope to enjoy its eventual beauty, I must provide each of these and not neglect it.

The same is true of our spiritual growth. We rest in the "soil" of Jesus when He becomes our personal Savior, but we wither if we don't nurture that relationship. It needs regular feeding. If we are to mature on this faith journey and come to the image of the Savior we profess, there are protocols we must employ regularly. We languish if we neglect the reading and study of God's Word; if we fail to pray; if we do not actively seek His discernment and the leading of the Holy Spirit; if we forego fellowship with other believers who both encourage and hold us accountable for our actions. Spiritual growth requires "good soil," the kind Jesus describes in Luke 8:15 [NRSV] when He said, *"But as for that in the good soil, these are the ones who, when they hear the word, hold it fast in an honest and good heart, and bear fruit with patient endurance."* Hearing God's Word, holding fast to it, and allowing it to bear fruit are the necessary ingredients for eventual spiritual growth. Believers who utilize them are like my amaryllis bulb that slowly and surely assumes the look and characteristics of the plant it is meant to be; one that gives joy and delight to those who gaze upon it. These believers move from their "bulb stage" to eventual spiritual maturity relying upon God's growing strategies. They bring similar joy and delight as the image of Christ shines in and through them.

CHAPTER 18

A PASS

Rifling through my journals of recent years, I happened upon an entry I penned in one of them on March 24, 2017. At the time, I was living in the house that Earl had had built as our retirement dream home with my only son, my daughter-in-law, and three of my four grandchildren. My soulmate did not get to enjoy his dream house very long. For reasons only He knows, the Lord summoned him home less than three years after it was completed. It was a huge place; and with its ample living spaces, it made sense for my son and family to share with me its comforts and amenities. Eight years had passed since Earl's transition to heaven when I wrote the following:

Coming into the house recently after having survived one of those days that tests one's endurance, I met QE on his way to an evening program at his school where he was to recite a monologue. Surprised, as the event was news to me, I said to him, "I wish I had known about tonight."

Peering up at me as he tied his shoes, he replied, "You're coming, aren't you?"

"Well," I stammered, "You know I always like to attend your events. Do you want me to come?"

He paused and then looking me directly in the eye answered, "Do you want to come?" And then without allowing me to respond went on to say, "That's ok, Nyanya (Swahili for grandmother), you can have a pass tonight."

I thought about our exchange a few days later. This eight-year-old grandson, born the year following Earl's death and the bearer of his grandfather's middle name, had sensed my conflicting desires at the moment of our exchange—me tired and wanting nothing more than to rest on one hand and on the other, not wishing to miss seeing him perform as I usually do. Saving me from having to make a decision, he gave me a pass. A gift of grace to his beloved Nyanya.

Isn't that what God does? He sees us navigate life, earnestly most times trying to steer in the right direction, to keep afloat and not be swept under by life's everchanging currents. He understands our frustrations, our conflicting emotions, our indecisive moments, our humanness. And then when we least expect Him to, rather than watch us squirm as we struggle to make the best choices, He simply says,

> *"Come to me all you who are weary and burdened and I will give you rest."*
>
> ~Matthew 11:28

In essence, God gives us a pass. We don't have to struggle to make the right decision. We can go to Him and find the answers He would have us receive.

QE's pass was a release from my anxiety over the dilemma of the moment. God's pass is the peace He gives when we accept His promises to meet us in the moments of our dilemmas; and to guide us in the direction we should go.

CHAPTER 19

JIGSAWS AND LIFE

One of my favorite Christmas gifts last month was a 500-piece jigsaw puzzle. The giver, a dear sister-friend, had it made from a picture I'd sent her that my daughter-in-law snapped as my grandson and I walked in a parking lot. It captured one of those precious grandmother-grandchild moments that fill our memory banks. As an avid jigsaw puzzle fan, I am at present enjoying the challenge of putting it together; fitting the small pieces to form the image of the photo that brings a smile each time I glance at it. It's a time-consuming pastime; one that requires patience, a good eye, dogged perseverance and acceptance that on some days victory may be finding just one piece that fits! Puzzle aficionados also accept the reality that completing a puzzle may take weeks, sometimes months. The key to completion is in direct correlation to the amount of time devoted to trying the pieces to see if they fit. The last puzzle I completed took me two months. I've taken to framing them now to give as gifts; though in this case this one will adorn the wall in the bedroom my grandson claims as *his room*.

In addition to stimulating the brain cells and exercising the fingers, jigsaw puzzles also provide quiet time for reflection. That realization came to me yesterday, and I received it as a thought from the Lord that He wishes me to share. Hence "Jigsaws and Life." As believers we accept that our lives are not random; that God had, when He allowed our conception and birth, an image of who we were to be and a design for the life we were to eventually live. A life that worshipped and glorified Him above all else. And although He created us for Himself, He did not make us robots. He gave us free-will; the ability to choose whether who we became as adults reflects the image He imagined for us; or not. From the moment we come to know and accept Him as Savior, the pieces of who we are should begin coming together into the image of Christ whom we seek to imitate.

Notice that I said "should." Our reality as humans is that the pieces of who we are and who God created us to be don't always align. And as we live, too often the effort to fit them together into His design seems more and more an impossibility. You may feel, like I do on those days when no matter how long I stare at the puzzle pieces, pick them up, or move them from one spot to another, they don't fit. But I've discovered the key to puzzle completion. Without fail when I take some time away from the puzzle table, and focus on other things, inevitably when I return in the next day or two, my eye hones in on those pesky pieces, and I'll see exactly where one or two of them should be placed.

I purport the same can be true in life. When its pieces are all over the place; when nothing is as it ought to be; when everything you've tried has failed; when your prayers bounce off the wall; when it seems that it can't get any worse, perhaps it's time to step away. Maybe God is calling you to rest a moment; to both read and reflect upon His Word; to pray only prayers of thanksgiving without mentioning a need or a want; to bask in the silence of time alone with Him, allowing His spirit to soak deeply into the turmoil of your mind. Maybe we get so engrossed in figuring out where everything ought to go or how everything ought to be, we lose sight of the big picture, and our efforts to make our life pieces fit come to naught. Perhaps life's completed jigsaw in the design God drew looks like this:

"She had a sister called Mary, who sat at the Lord's feet listening to what he said... Martha was distracted by all the preparations that had to be made. She came to him and asked, "Lord, don't you care that my sister has left me to do the work by myself? Tell her to help me!' 'Martha, Martha,' the Lord answered, 'you are worried and upset about many things, but only one thing is needed. Mary has chosen what is better, and it will not be taken away from her.'"
~Luke 10:39–42

The picture of Mary sitting at Jesus' feet, unhurried and unworried, at peace in that moment as she listens and allows His words to shape who she is and can be is a snapshot of what it means to come into the image of the one who created us. For only in the state Mary chose will the irregularly shaped pieces of our lives have the potential to form the full portrait of the image of Christ in us. Now, that's a jigsaw puzzle worth all the time and effort it takes to complete and frame!

CHAPTER 20

GOD'S CONDITIONAL PROMISES

"Standing on the promises of Christ my King
Through eternal ages, let his praises ring
Glory in the highest, I will shout and sing
Standing on the promise of God
Standing, standing, standing on the promises of God, my Savior
Standing, standing, I'm standing on the promises of God."

If you're Protestant by faith, and attended (or attend) church worship services, you are probably familiar with the lyrics of this gospel hymn written by Russell Kelso Carter, a professor in the Pennsylvania Military College of Chester. While there he was licensed to preach by the Methodist Episcopal Church and was quite active in leading camp meetings and revivals. Eventually, poor health forced him to abandon this work, and he turned his attention to the study of medicine and became a physician and a writer. He wrote novels as well as hymns. More often than not, *Standing on the Promises* finds worshippers rising to their feet as they sing this congregational hymn. It is an expression of their faith in God and His promises to them.

This foundational understanding of our faith—God's multiple promises to those who believe in Him and the tenets of Christianity—helps believers in their day-to-day journey and efforts to live a Christlike life. On an elementary level, it's simple. The Bible speaks to His promises, and we receive that word in faith, that what He says He will do. A recent quote in a devotional I read gave me pause; setting in motion this reflective piece. The author penned, *"Many of God's promises are conditional requiring some initial action on our part.*" I confess I had not thought of them from that perspective. I was of the school that a promise is a promise. Needless to say, I've discovered there is truth in that assertion; and if, as Charles Stanley writes, "*the Lord's priority is our spiritual development,*" it's reasonable to assume we must look beyond the elementary if we are to mature in our faith.

The Bible is dotted with examples of God's promises to us that require something from us for those promises to be delivered. In the book of Genesis, God promises to make of Abram (Abraham) a great nation, to bless him and make his name great if he leaves his country and family and goes to an unknown land which the Lord will show him. The delivery of that promise was set in motion only when as the Bible says,

> "*So Abram left, as the Lord had told him…*"
> ~Genesis 12:4

It was only after the priests carrying the ark stepped into the Jordan River which the Israelites had to cross to get to the land God had promised them did the water upstream stopped flowing, allowing the people to cross over. The promise was fulfilled *after* they placed their feet in the river. (Joshua 4:14–16) When Moses and the people fleeing Egypt were seemingly trapped by the sea blocking their passage, God said to Moses,

> "*Why are you crying out to me? Tell the Israelites to move on.*"
> ~Exodus 14:15

As they did so, God saved them from Pharaoh's pursuing army; the promise of God's deliverance activated by their obedience to stop lamenting and move on. Ten lepers met Jesus on His way to Jerusalem and cried out to Him,

> "*Jesus, Master, have pity on us.!' When he saw them, he said, 'Go, show yourselves to the priests.' And as they went, they were cleansed.*"
> ~Luke 17:13-14

Their prayer for healing was answered only after they did as Jesus instructed—"Go."

Lest these examples leave you thinking God's conditional promises are dramatic events of days long ago, reflect upon the following scriptures that suggest otherwise. Each illustrates God's promise with a condition for its realization. The promises are timeless; we can stand on them with surety. The only requirement for fulfillment is that we be both hearers and doers of His word.

> *"For God so loved the world that he gave his one and only Son, that whoever believes in him shall not perish but have eternal life."*
> ~John 3:16

His promise of eternal life contingent upon one's belief in Jesus.

> *"That if you confess with your mouth, 'Jesus is Lord,' and believe in your heart that God raised him from the dead, you will be saved."*
> ~Romans 10:9

The promise of salvation contingent upon confession and belief.

> *"You will keep in perfect peace him whose mind is steadfast, because he trusts in you."*
> ~Isaiah 26:3

The promise of peace contingent upon a steadfast mind.

> *"If you remain in me, and my words remain in you, ask whatever you wish and it will be given to you."*
> ~John15:7

The promise of receiving what we ask contingent upon remaining faithful to Jesus and allowing His word to live in us.

> *"but those who hope in the Lord will renew their strength. They will soar on wings like eagles; they will run and not grow weary; they will walk and not faint."*
> ~Isaiah 40:31

The promise of renewed strength contingent upon hope.

"Trust in the Lord with all your heart and lean not on your own understanding; in all your ways acknowledge him and he will make your paths straight."

~Proverbs 3:5–6

The promise of God's guidance in all things contingent upon trusting Him and not oneself.

Yes, God is faithful to His promises, and we can *take them to the bank.* But the mark of spiritual maturity requires we read the fine print of His words, mindful that sometimes we are called to activate the promise covenant.

CHAPTER 21

GOD'S UNCONDITIONAL LOVE

In the preceding chapter, I offered my rationale for asserting that some of God's promises are conditional. But gentle reader, please don't in the vernacular of the times, *get it twisted*. Though some of His promises may be conditional, nothing is conditional about God's love. Even if the Bible were bereft of His promises to us, it would not alter the reality of His love for us. In other words, whether He made promises or not, God loved what He created—the world and all therein.

The expression of His love is the foundation of our relationship with Him. Thousands of years before Jesus even spoke these words—*"For God so loved the world that he gave his one and only Son, that whoever believes in him shall not perish but have eternal life."* (John 3:16)—God had demonstrated time and time again that He loved humanity, even when it failed to love Him in return.

"I have loved you with an everlasting love," He declares in Jeremiah 31:3. *"The earth is full of his unfailing love," "Your love, O Lord reaches to the heavens," "The Lord is compassionate and gracious, slow to anger, abounding in love,"* the writer of Psalms pens. And in the years following Jesus' resurrection and ascension, the disciples and apostles continued to write of God's love for us as they spread the gospel of that love throughout the known world. *"This is how God showed his love among us: He sent his one and only Son into the world that we live through him. This is love: not that we loved God, but He loved us and sent his son as an atoning sacrifice for our sins,"* writes the Apostle John. The words of the most prolific biblical New Testament witnesses acclaims, *"But because of his great love us, God who is rich in mercy, made us alive with Christ even when we were dead in transgressions…"*

And though some may suggest otherwise, God loves us still. In a 21st century world filled with sin, the God who created us continues to seek us, and to bring us back into right relationship with Him. From a secular perspective it might seem we should be abandoned to our depravity; but God continues to show His love through the extension of His mercy, grace, and favor. Yes, today, right now God loves us unconditionally. That, too, we can *take to the bank*.

CHAPTER 22

RUIN
The Road to Transformation

I appropriated the title of this piece from Elizabeth Gilbert's memoir, *Eat Pray Love*, that was made into a movie of the same name. *"Ruin,"* she wrote, *"is the road to transformation."* The sentiment captured my imagination; it seemed a somewhat oxymoronic idea that ruin, which we usually think of as devastation, irreparable damage, or shattered hopes and dreams, would lead to transformation, which we equate with renewal or conversion. If something or someone is ruined, we don't hold out much hope that anything good can emerge from the ruination. No, the tendency is to consign whatever or whoever is ruined to the garbage dump or landfill; to the hovels that house the hopeless, to the fringes of life; preferably out of sight.

I've forgotten how this quote was acted out in the movie, but it has stayed with me. The concept is biblical in some ways—devastation leading to transformation. The Old Testament's familiar story of Joseph, and his progression from favored son to Egyptian slave is a perfect example. His life was shattered when his brothers sold him into slavery. And though initially, he enjoyed his master's favor, when he was falsely accused of inappropriate behavior with the wife of Potiphar, his ruin seemed sealed. Yet, as scripture relates, the road that led to his eventual transformation from prisoner to governor of Egypt would not have occurred had he not first known the devastation of family betrayal and slavery.

The Apostle Paul's story too can be viewed through a similar lens. A Roman citizen from the upper echelons of society, educated, respected within his community, and a fierce zealot in the persecution of the Jews who were converts to the early Christian church, his privileged position and dreams for greater conquests came to naught on that Damascus Road. In an instance, he lost his eyesight; his plans were shattered; he became dependent upon others to take him to the home of one of the very individuals who he had set out to take captive. That moment of ruin became for the man Saul the road that led to his transformation into one of God's anointed. He would become the Apostle to the Gentiles who spread the Gospel of Jesus Christ throughout the Roman empire.

This idea that ruin can be turned into renewal is not reserved for biblical times. It is a theme applicable to all who believe in the power of God's grace—and His favor. We do not have to settle for those times in life's journey when ruin stops our progression: sickness, losses of any kind, dreams dashed; plans foiled, by others or by ourselves; natural disasters; manmade disasters; even death. No matter the face ruin wears, behind it is a path, a way that, with God's guidance and divine intervention, can point us in a new direction; a direction we would not have taken or known had we not faced the ruin that befell us. A direction that transforms us into the man or woman whom our Creator birthed us to be.

CHAPTER 23

HUMANITY PLANS. GOD SMILES.

I believe a disclaimer or two may be appropriate as I begin. There is nothing inherently wrong with the concept of planning. I believe God values order, rather than chaos. We can look at the creation story and see a model of an orderly process achieving a desired result; that's planning. This reflection stems more from the perspective of us forgetting who we are; and who God is. In the creation of humankind in His image, God chose to give us minds of our own rather than have us roam around as His robots or drones. We have what we term *free-will*. And it is the exercise of our free-will that gets us into trouble; that places us in situations which illustrate my title.

Let's begin with Psalm 20, a petitionary psalm attributed to King David. Verse 4 reads, *"May he give you the desire of your heart and make all your plans succeed."* It's easy to conclude from this kingly request that one of humanity's expectations of God is that He is in our life to grant our desires and make our plans successful; emphasis upon *our*. As we mature in faith, we come to understand that the desires of our heart must align with God's desires, and our plans must be within His design for our life. Perhaps that is why Solomon writes in the Book of Proverbs, *"In his heart a man plans his course, but the Lord determines his steps,"* (Proverbs 16:9); and *"Commit to the Lord whatever you do, and your plans will succeed."* (Proverbs 16:3) Both of these scriptures clarify our roles. God is God; we are human. When with our free-will, we cross the line that distinguishes who's who, we place ourselves center stage where His *smile* lights upon us; and where, too, I imagine He shakes His head as He goes about sorting out the chaos we've created.

The Lord declares in Isaiah 55, verses 8–9, *"As the heavens are higher than the earth, so are my ways higher than your ways and my thoughts than your thoughts."* The Apostle James writes, *"Now listen, you who say, 'Today or tomorrow we will go to this or that city, spend a year there, carry on business and make money.' Why, you do not even know what will happen tomorrow. What is your life? You are a mist that appears for a little while and then vanishes. Instead, you ought to say, 'If it is the Lord's will, we will live and do this or that.'"* (James 4:13–15) The more we study God's word, the clearer the delineation of our relationship with Him becomes. Passages such as these help us move toward that image of humanity He intended; and move away from the one we've crafted ourselves. *"Many are the plans in a man's heart, but it is the Lord's purpose that prevails."* (Proverbs 19:21) And finally, again, perhaps the most familiar and trustworthy verse of this book of adages that offer advice for living so that one's plans are in concert with Gods;

> *"Trust in the Lord with all your heart and lean not on your own understanding; in all your ways acknowledge him, and he will make your path straight."*
>
> ~Proverbs 3:5–6

May His smile be one of approval when you set about your planning because you begin it with Him.

CHAPTER 24

Good Trouble

I've been wondering if when he penned the tweet below in June 2018, the former Baptist minister and iconic civil rights leader, the now-departed Congressman John Lewis knew it would become an oxymoronic phrase of contemporary speech. *"Be hopeful, be optimistic,"* he tweeted. *"Our struggle is not the struggle of a day, a week, a month, or a year, it is the struggle of a lifetime. Never, ever be afraid to make some noise and get in good trouble, necessary trouble."* What was he thinking as he issued this clarion call for those engaged in the ongoing struggle for social justice in the nation and the world? Surely, he knew many would scratch their heads or wrinkle their brows as they pondered the incongruity of "good and necessary trouble." After all, we don't think of trouble as something good or necessary; quite the opposite—something to be avoided if at all possible. Lately, I came to the conclusion that what the congressman was advocating is nothing new; that he is not the originator of the "theology of good and necessary trouble." And because of his religious training and faith traditions, what inspired him to tweet that message is in essence biblical. Who after all better modeled getting into good and necessary trouble than Jesus? Who other than He was unafraid to make some noise?

Now this perspective may take some persuasion, so let me go directly to our source document, God's holy Word the Bible, to offer a few illustrations of Jesus moving about the Holy Land in His day, demonstrating, agitating, getting in trouble with the authorities and religious leaders of that time. If we understand that getting into "good" and "necessary" trouble means challenging the status quo, addressing societal injustices, caring for the least, the weakest and neediest amongst us through our actions and utilization of our God-given talents and resources to do so, then it's clear that what scripture recounts of Jesus' three years ministry personifies just that. For a moment, let's travel in time to some of those scenes in that ministry when, as recorded throughout the Gospels, we see the originator of the "Good and Necessary Trouble" theology in action. As He spoke to the crowd on that mountainside as recorded in the early chapters of Matthew's Gospel, much of what He said defied the social and religious traditions. Many of His "You have heard that it was said," teachings flew in the face of religious and civic leaders. And as this first "rally" ended, we can hear the people speak of this man who spoke so fervently, unlike the teachers of the law. At another time when Jesus had returned to the town, *"Some men brought to him a paralytic, lying on a mat. When Jesus saw their faith, he said to the paralytic, 'Take heart, son; your sins are forgiven.' At this, some of the teachers of the law said to themselves, 'This fellow is blaspheming.'"* Jesus of course knew what they were thinking and proceeded to push the envelope even further. In a demonstration of who He was, He commanded the paralytic to get up, take his mat and go home. Such a public display of His power was surely an egregious insult to the teachers, elders, Pharisees and Sadducees. The line was drawn; a movement launched. Heading that movement was the One who had been sent with a specific purpose: the atonement of humankind's sin through His death on a cross. To accomplish His purpose would require Him to engage in *"good and necessary trouble."*

The other Gospels are replete with Jesus' radical activism. Walking through grainfields one Sabbath, He and the disciples picked some heads of grain and began to eat them. The Pharisees immediately challenged Him: *"Look, why are they doing what is unlawful on the Sabbath?"* According to the law, working on the Sabbath was forbidden. Picking the grain heads was equated with working, so they violated the law by so doing. After reminding the supposed teachers of the law of what the Torah read about what David and his men did when they were hungry, Jesus said,

"The Sabbath was made for man, not man for the Sabbath. So, the Son of Man is Lord even of the Sabbath."

~Mark 2:23-27

On another occasion Jesus saw a tax collector named Levi who He called to follow Him. Levi left everything and did so. When Levi threw a great banquet at his house for Jesus, tax collectors and others were included among the guests. Observing the festivities, the teachers of the law and Pharisees challenged Jesus. *"Why do you eat and drink with tax collectors and sinners?"* The question may be asked from our 21st century perspective why they were even at Levi's house in the first place. Obviously, they weren't invited. But their presence did provide Jesus another opportunity to challenge their religiosity; to refuse to accept their biases as a norm; and do to so openly for all to witness. (Like 5:27–31) Perhaps the most vivid picture of Jesus as an agitator for change willing to make some noise and get in good, necessary trouble is that of him entering the temple in Jerusalem after His triumphal entry the day before. Going into the temple area, He:

> *"...began driving out those who were buying and selling there. He overturned the tables of the money changers and the benches of those selling doves"* (one of those moments in our day when the police would be called to apprehend the culprit in the act of destroying private property). *He further prevented anyone from carrying merchandise through the temple courts, saying as He taught them, "Is it not written: My house will be called a house of prayer for all nations."*
>
> ~Mark 11:15-17

Cleansing the temple of commercialism in an era when it served as a religious marketplace, filled with shysters and racketeers was the epitome of someone who intentionally gets into "good trouble." No shrinking violet was this Jesus on a mission to restore God's vision for the world He created. Changing hearts and minds required nothing less. There is no fear of consequences. Through a "good and necessary trouble" lens one sees what needs to be done and does it. As Congressman Lewis noted, the struggle for justice is the struggle of a lifetime. Isaiah tells us, *"For the Lord is a God of justice."* And God speaks through his prophet Amos, *"But let justice roll on like a river, righteousness like a never-ending stream."* Jesus gave us the example of what addressing humanity's ongoing struggles looks like. It's why He is the New Testament originator of protest movements. Congressman Lewis' call seems to simply say: *Do what Jesus did. Make some noise. Get in some good, necessary trouble. Do it for a lifetime.*

CHAPTER 25

When You've Done All You Can

It dawned upon me after I typed the title for this chapter; which ironically, I had selected even before I wrote the preceding one, that this chapter could be viewed as contradictory of the ideas of its predecessor. Had I stumbled into a quagmire of my own making? If I had, was there a way out in which I could solidify both perspectives? As a writer of Christian themes, I reached for my primary source material. The Bible would show me the way forward. Reflect with me as we substantiate that the former chapter's theme in no way negates this one. Rather they work together to show how we 21st believers in Jesus Christ should be living His teachings.

The title of this chapter is taken from the opening lyrics of a popular gospel song sung most familiarly by gospel singer, Donnie McClurkin, titled "Stand," which ponders what to do when it feels like no matter how much you have accomplished, it is simply not enough. It's a question we can assume the sick woman in Mark's Gospel had asked countess times.

> *"And a woman was there who had been subject to bleeding for twelve years. She suffered a great deal under the care of many doctors and had spent all she had, yet instead of getting better she grew worse. When she heard about Jesus, she came up behind him in the crowd and touched his cloak, because she thought, 'If I just touch his clothes, I will be healed.' Immediately her bleeding stopped and she felt in her body that she was freed from her suffering... 'Who touched my clothes,' Jesus asked. 'Who touched me?' Then the woman, knowing what had happened to her, came and fell at his feet, and trembling*

with fear, told him the whole truth. He said to her, 'Daughter, your faith has healed you. Go in peace and be freed from your suffering.'"
~Mark 5:25–34

All you can do when what you can do is not enough is stand through it all, keep holding on, don't give up and allow God to step in, the lyrist admonishes. The sick woman had exhausted her resources seeing doctors whose treatments failed to alleviate her condition. Now 12 years and counting, she decides to place herself in a position that challenges the mores of her times. In her *unclean* condition, she should not have even been in the crowd, but isolated in her home. Yet, there she was, risking everything, getting into good trouble; knowing this was the right time. It was a now-or- never moment as she stretched her hand to touch the hem of the garment of this man Jesus. In that simple gesture hope and faith resided. She'd done all she could and then some, as she refused to bow to the conventions of the day. In keeping with the lyrics, she simply stood, and God rewarded her faith. He healed her.

Implicit in this message is the reality of what goes before the *standing*. Humanity's struggles are lifelong. They ebb and flow throughout the seasons. Pain, grief, injustice, sorrow, sickness. Tears and prayers dot the map of the journey through them all. But we refuse to give despair the victory. We "make some noise; get in some good trouble;" we pray, and when we realize we've done all we can, we put whatever it is in our too *big-for-me basket*, get out of His way, and let God be God. Standing on the sidelines, we watch Him exert His power and bring about His purposes.

CHAPTER 26

ARE YOU READY?

No one was more adept at knowing one's audience than Jesus. The Gospels abound with the parables He spoke in the vernacular and experiences of the people during that age. My quirky mind often lands upon a particular story that shouts to be reframed in contemporary speak. Such is the case with Jesus' Parable of the Ten Virgins. In private, the disciples had asked Him to explain the signs of His return—The Second Coming—and the end of the age. (Matthew 24:1-3) Following a lengthy discourse, He told them the coming of the arrival of the new kingdom would be similar to that of ten maidens being prepared and ready for the arrival of the bridegroom whom they were to accompany into the wedding banquet. All 10 of them had their lamps ready to shine upon him as he approached, but only five had remembered to bring extra oil to keep the lamps burning. Jesus called the five who forgot their oil *foolish*, and the five who remembered *wise*. After a long wait, the bridegroom arrived. The wise maidens' lamps blazed brightly as they entered the hall with him. Alas, not so with the foolish ones. They missed the bridegroom because they were away trying to buy the oil they should have had. When they returned, the scripture reads;

"Later the others came. 'Sir! Sir!' they said, 'Open the door for us!' But he replied, 'I tell you the truth, I don't know you.' Therefore, keep watch, because you do not know the day or the hour.'"
~Matthew 25:1-13

Just in case you missed the point of the parable, here it is. The bridegroom represents Jesus' second coming—His return and the celebration that event will usher in. The wise maidens are those who will be ready for His return. The foolish maidens are those who will not be ready.

For some of you, this might be a stretch, but as I visualize the wise maidens holding their lamps up high to light their way, to use them to see the bridegroom make his way forward and into the banquet hall, I can't help reframing that scene in today's world. Those lamps would be the ubiquitous cell phone, camera pointing upward as the clouds unfold, and the Savior appears. Those who keep their phones charged (with a wireless charger as backup) would not miss the glory of that moment. And the others whose phones seem always to be about to lose power will bemoan that and the fact that their spare charger is at home.

Lest someone misses the point of the parable as Jesus told it or as I reframed it, let's allow scripture to give further clarity. In chapter 13 of the Gospel of Mark, Jesus tells the disciples to keep watch; no one knows except God when He will return. *"What I say to you, I say to everyone: Watch."* As the writer of Luke in chapter 21 records, Jesus said to his followers, *"Be careful, or your hearts will be weighed down with dissipation, drunkenness and the anxieties of life, and that day will close on you like a trap. For it will come upon all those who live on the face of the whole earth. Be always on the watch, and pray that you may be able to escape all that is about to happen, and that you may be able to stand before the Son of Man."* We who profess Christ proclaim the mystery of faith: *"Christ has died. Christ has risen. Christ will come again."* And we understand that when He does return, we must be ready to do more than jostle to get just the right picture of Him; but to welcome Him and be invited by Him to the great banquet He has prepared. Being ready requires us to be watchful in everything. What we watch, what we speak, what we think, what we read, what we give, what we withhold, what we share, what we serve, what we value, how we spend our time, on what we spend our resources. Being ready is constantly watching; correcting what we see if it doesn't conform to Jesus' teachings and commands; striving daily by His grace to answer that question with a resounding, "Yes, I am ready."

CHAPTER 27

OUR EYES ARE UPON YOU

This was not the reflective piece I had chosen for this chapter. But when I sat down to write, the words of Jehoshaphat, the king of Jerusalem circa 870–849 BCE, for some reason tumbled through my mind.

> *"We do not know what to do, but our eyes are on you."*
> ~2 Chronicles 20:12

Perhaps the statement resonates because of what currently has the world's attention in Europe: the massive Russian army bombing its way into the country of Ukraine, bent upon the overthrow of that nation. It's an easy juxtaposition—the people of Judah and Jerusalem facing off against an enemy that outnumbered them; *"O our God, will you not judge them? For we have no power to face this vast army that is attacking us."* and the people of Ukraine caught in the crosshairs of an enemy they feel is much too powerful for them to engage. And though the Ukrainian president to our knowledge has not uttered the words of Jehoshaphat, it's not a stretch to think he may have had similar thoughts as this European conflict continues to rage. As an Orthodox Christian, he most surely is seeking not just secular guidance, but spiritual as well as he faces the forces of evil attacking his country. The words of the ancient biblical king ring with the same urgency today as they did when he spoke them nearly three millennia ago. On the world's stage, we find ourselves admitting our dependency (whether aloud or silently) upon God as our solution to this threat that reaches beyond the continent in which it occurs. As scripture proclaims, what He spoke to the people in those ancient times, He speaks still to us, *"For the battle is not yours, but the Lord's."*

That divine assurance is as applicable today as it was in 870 BCE. And though I've referenced it in a conflict of gargantuan proportions, it is also relevant in circumstances that may seem insignificant in comparison. Let's be honest, in our everyday trials and challenges, often we reach the point where we think or say, *"I don't know what to do."* But how many of us can say we add the ending, *"but my eyes are on you."* I venture not all that many. More likely we turn first to family, friends, co-workers, trusted confidants, perhaps even the preacher for help in dealing with the issue; and to be clear, I'm not suggesting there is something wrong with seeking advice from these sources. But I believe for those of us who claim His name, our default position in every situation is God. Calling on Him to be the *first responder* in times of danger, difficulty, or uncertainty validates our trust and belief in Him. We affirm our faith with this simple declaration and acknowledge that in our own strength we can do nothing. For truly, within both the ordinary and the extraordinary situations that we label *life*; the good, the bad, and the ugly we term *the human experience*, ultimately, we must pause and hear Him say to us, *"This battle is not yours, but mine."*

"Come to me, all you who are weary and burdened, and I will give you rest."

~Matthew 11:28

As it spoke to our biblical ancestors, scripture speaks to us in this year of our Lord, 2022. Our eyes are on our Savior; there is no one else on whom we can focus in times such as these. So, we look to Him, listen for the leading of His Spirit for what He would have us to do; and then release to Him the outcomes. The battle is His.

"Look to the Lord and his strength; seek his face always."

~1 Chronicles 16:11

CHAPTER 28

ACROSS THE RIVER
"If Only" to "No More" Land

In a land long forgotten lived a people who dreamed that one day they would reap the benefits of a life well-lived. Diligently they went about the everyday activities in which humans engage. They worked, some for themselves; others for someone else. They nurtured and raised families. They were teachers, physicians, lawyers, business-women and men, professional sports players, scientists, clergymen and women, therapists, electricians, plumbers, artists, actors and actresses. In other words, they were people like people have been since the earth was peopled. (The play on words is deliberate!)

In that land in which they lived and worked ran a long, wide river, known to them as the river "If Only." It flowed swiftly and served as a barrier to what lay beyond. The people had been taught from childhood that on the other side of the river was a place called "No More" land. The elders spun tales of the delights awaiting anyone who succeeded in getting across to it. But in all the ages the people had resided along the river banks, no one knew of anyone who had done so. When the children would ask their parents and grand-parents why no one ever had, their responses always began with an explanation prefaced by the phrase "If only."

"If only we had the right boat."

"If only the weather wasn't so bad."

"If only we had the time."

"If only my work didn't require my attention."

"If only there were more hours in the day."

Though the people couldn't see the land's delights and pleasures, they were certain that they existed. And as far as we know, they continued living within reach of their dreams, but they were held hostage by their excuses and so never realized them.

There is a lesson in this little tale for all who profess Christ and hope to one day know the joy of eternity with Him. Far too many of us never know the abundant life God intended when He allowed our birth. Once we leave the innocence of childhood, He gives us opportunities to make choices to navigate life's journey toward its final destination: eternity and life in His presence. Those choice-making times arise when situations and circumstances bring us to the banks of the river "If Only." And like the people in our tale, we often forfeit what awaits us in the here and now and hereafter, rooted in indecision, fear, uncertainty, ignorance, apathy, faithlessness, and unbelief.

For many of us, it takes little effort to recall those "if only" seasons of life.

If only I had stayed in school and earned my degree, who knows how God could have used me.

If only I had listened to the counselor, my parents, my pastor when that door opened and I chose not to walk through it.

If only I had spent more time studying my Bible, attending church, praying.

If only I had followed the doctor's advice and changed my diet. If only I had quit smoking.

If only.

God created us with free will. The moments that demand the exercise of it are the moments when we either stand on the river bank, mumbling our "if only" excuse, or we step out in faith that what's on the other side is worth the risk, worth taking the stance that challenges the tenor of the times, worth saying, "Yes," to God and, "No," to the world.

Our Creator prewired us to long for what awaits in the Land of "No More" in the hereafter. And because He knows our frailty and propensity toward sin, He designed the human journey such that the experiences, situations, and circumstances we encounter grow that sense of longing. We were created also with free will, to make choices that have potential to help us avoid the universal "No Mores" of our inhumanity toward one another in the present. In this life and the hoped-for life ever after, the choices are ours to make. Will we choose to be held hostage by excuses that begin with "if only," or will we break the bonds that keep us from God's favor and blessings and know the joy, peace and prosperity of both the temporal and eternal lands of "no more?"

CHAPTER 29

Toolbox for the Times

"For everything there is a season, and a time for every matter under heaven."

~Ecclesiastes 3:1 [NRSV]

When we think of a toolbox, more often than not, the image of a red, orange, or black chest filled with assorted tools that has its set place in a garage or toolshed comes to mind. My husband had several of them—one of which I kept. Handyman that he was, he made certain that no matter the need or problem, the appropriate tool was within reach to deal with it. New furniture or toys needing assembly—a screwdriver was his tool of choice. An overflowing toilet—his pliers gripped what needed gripping to make the repair. Hanging pictures—the lever positioned and the hammer drove in the hanging nail. Estimating spaces for planting the annual flowerbeds—his ever-ready tape measure informed his decisions. Rope was cut with the utility knife that hung on his work pants. A missing bolt or nut was replaced with a wrench; wood was cut with a handsaw; a mallet knocked wooden pieces together. And his flashlight lighted the darkness of the crawl space underneath the house when he had to connect the exterior Christmas lights. No matter the reason or the season, Earl's toolbox contained the tools that he needed to address the matter.

In a similar fashion, we live in times that bombard us with one problem after another. Grief still consumes the many who lost loved ones to a 21st century pandemic that upended our sense of normal. Even as it appears the worse may be behind us, the tragedy of COVID-19 stalks us; uncertainty seems to reign. The unrelenting sin of the race-based caste system endemic to our country remains either ignored or sanitized. Our children continue to grow up in an environment that abuses, neglects, or victimizes them. Our elderly struggle for dignity and compassionate care in far too many places. After four years of warped government which we strive to reverse, division and ugliness mark us a people who belie who we proclaim to be. To whom do we turn? To what? Scripture tells believers that we do not conform to the world; that though we live in the world, we are not of the world. How do we live those beliefs in this season, in this time? We reach inside our toolbox—God's sacred Word. Everything that we need to live without fear; to live with joy; to embrace His truths even when lies abound; to have a peace that surpasses all understanding; to grasp His omnipotence, omnipresence, and omniscience are contained therein.

When grief squeezes the heart and tears won't stop flowing, grasp the divine word pliers of Psalm 119:50 (*My comfort in my suffering is this: Your promise reserves my life.*), Psalm 23:4 (*Though I walk through the valley of the shadow of death, I will fear no evil; for you are with me; your rod and your staff comfort me.*), Lamentations 3:22 (*Because of the Lord's great love, we are not consumed. Great is His faithfulness.*), and Revelation 21:4 (*He will wipe every tear from their eyes. There will be on more death or mourning or crying or pain, for the old order of things has passed away.*) When the will to speak truth in combat against social inequities and the inhumane treatment and care of the most vulnerable amongst us weakens, pick up the screwdrivers of Proverbs 3:5–6 (*Trust in the Lord with all your heart and lean not on your own understanding; in all your ways acknowledge him and He will make your paths straight.*), Romans 8:28 (*And we know that in all things God works for the good of those who love Him, who have been called according to His purpose.*), Galatians 6:9 (*Let us not grow weary in doing good, for at the proper time we will reap a harvest if we do not give up.*), Psalm 27:13-14 (*I am still confident of this: I will see the goodness of the Lord in the land of the living. Wait for the Lord; be strong and take courage and wait for the Lord.*); Hebrews 11:1 (*Now faith is being sure of what we hope for and certain of what we do not see.*) Let the flashlight of Isaiah 26:3 (*You will keep in perfect peace him whose mind is steadfast, because he trusts in you.*) and Mark 12:30–31(*Love the Lord your God with all your heart and with all your soul and with all your mind and with all your strength. The second is this: Love your neighbor as yourself. There is no commandment greater than these.*) shine in your persona and behaviors, giving witness to your faith.

The list of biblical tools is inexhaustible. They are containable within the Bible because they are represented by words. Imagine if it were otherwise, that each took a physical form. The size of a toolbox to contain them would rival the Seven Wonders of the World! The next time you are feeling discouraged, overwhelmed, depressed, worried, uncertain, or just facing the ordinary complexities life presents, take a moment to grab your biblical toolbox. Go to your quiet time spot with a comfy throw, and settle in for some *lap time* with the One to whom the world and everyone in it belongs.

CHAPTER 30

URGENCY REVISITED

I began this book two years ago with the chapter "The Urgency of Now." I am ending it with the realization that though steps in a better direction might have been made in some of the areas I raised as "urgent," much remains unresolved, ignored, or simply dismissed. Perhaps, more alarmingly, new issues have arisen that bring their own urgency to the table. Far be from me to end on an alarmist note. Christians, by definition as believers in and followers of Jesus, do not believe in alarmism. But it would be remiss of me if I did not speak truth to the tenor of our times two years hence, with the hope that in so doing, the prophesy of Isaiah 43:19 becomes our reality. *"See, I am doing a new thing! Now it springs up; do you not perceive it? I am making a way in the wilderness and streams in the wasteland."*

A little over 50 years ago, in 1970, to be exact, Bobby Seale, a leader of the Black Panthers, wrote a book entitled *Seize the Time*. It's one of many such books written during that turbulent era in our nation that find a home on my bookshelves. Silent sentinels, these volumes give witness to the as yet unresolved issues of our caste-based racial divide. Seale's book cover, with letters written in bold black on a white background, haunted me such that I toyed with the idea of using it for the title of this chapter. Today, as I finished a devotional and turned the page to tomorrow's message, the title of it leaped from the page. "No Time Like the Present" it read. *Indeed,* I thought. There is "no time like the present" to "seize the time" to be the people of God He created us to be.

Two years ago, two giants sprawled across the width and length of our nation: a racial divide undergirded by a centuries old caste system few understood or acknowledged and a viral invasion that threatened our way of life, our institutions, our mortality. As the reins of power passed January 2020, from one administration to the next, the nation reeled as one or the other of the giants taunted us; flaunting their seeming invincibility to our defensive efforts at containment or solution. Street protests and counter protests; vitriolic accusations of election fraud (with no proof thereof); extremists touting racial supremacy reminiscent of history's worst exhibitions of man's inhumanity to man; a virus decimating the health care system's ability to provide care; a frantic pursuit for a vaccine when it became apparent nothing in the medicinal armory was effective against COVID; a national daily death count streaming on television screens as the virus stomped and slashed its way throughout the land.

As I fore-stated, some progress has been made. In our nation and around the world, the viral giant has been stalled in its onslaught, if not completely conquered. Scientists and pharmaceutical companies rose to the occasion; concocting vaccines that arrested the virus' threat. The CDC and other governmental bodies instituted non-medicinal protocols to further slow the disease's spread. On the social front, the protests are fewer; some revisions in police policies have been instituted to combat police brutality; some states and communities have made efforts to correct past and present practices related to racial based caste systems. It would be easy, exhausted as we are with the challenges of these two years, to turn a blind eye during this lull in the storm. But those of us who have lived a while know a lull is not an end. It's a phase that occurs sometimes just before the storm kicks up again; often fiercer than it was the first time it struck. Such is the scenario today. Added to the wars against the viral and social pandemics is the recent war launched by the president of Russia against Ukraine, a democratic sovereign nation across its border. Weary, the world warily watches the destruction in Europe unfold, wondering (Heaven forbid) if this is a precursor to WWIII.

Though we aren't ready yet to sing the old gospel song, "*The storm is passing over, alleluia!*" this is the time for us to stand stronger than ever in our faith; for that faith to be our bulwark, our first response to the aforementioned "giants" in this moment in our history. Jesus told the parable of the wise and foolish builders in Matthew 7:24–27. The house of the wise builder was constructed upon rock, a firm foundation; it stood against the storm's raging. So must it be for we who profess Christ. If we are to challenge the giants of this age, our slingshot of choice must be Jesus. "*On Christ the solid rock we stand, all other ground is sinking sand.*" Thusly armed, we can follow as He leads, unafraid and trusting His word that tells us not to fear for He is with us. (Isaiah 41:10) Even as the urgency remains.

"Truth forever on the scaffold, Wrong forever on the throne, yet that scaffold sways the future, and behind the dim unknown standeth God within the shadow, keeping watch above his own."

~James Russell Lowell

Acknowledgements

Trust in the Lord with all your heart and lean not on your own understanding; in all your ways submit to him, and he will make your path straight.

~Proverbs 3:5-6

TGBTG! To God be the glory for allowing me to complete book number five. It has been a challenge to do so within the new norms created within the past two years. Between relocating from Georgia to Texas, the place of my birth and maturation until I moved away at age 24—a place for which I have had ambivalent feelings since the assassination of John Kennedy—waiting on the completion of the construction of a new home, coping with the impact of COVID and the social uprising spurred by race-based casteism, and to top it off, a surprise health challenge that sidelined me for more than a few months, it is a wonder I finished the book at all. I give the credit for being able to do all of it to God, my heavenly Father and Sustainer. He allowed me to rest from my labor just long enough before sending the Holy Spirit to buzz about my ears with inspiration, nudges, the right scriptures at the right time, the serendipitous experiences or passages in a devotional book, the casual comment from a friend or family member that was anything but casual to point me in the direction for the next chapter.

I was joined on this venture by my longtime friend and "sister by another mother," Ann Lloyd, who for yet the third time has served as my critical ear. She listens as I read the chapters; pointing out inconsistencies, correcting biblical references, offering suggestions and insight gained over her years as a Bible teacher and leader of biblical studies. I am indebted to her and thankful for her encouragement. Team A&B on the court again!

I remain forever grateful and appreciative of family members and friends near and far who continue to support my writing by purchasing and reading my books; and recommending them to others. My "Grand-Four," Logan, Jordan, Brooklin and Quentin Earl (QE) inspire me with joy. Thank you, precious ones. I love you. God loves you more.

I am thankful that at this writing my one and only son, Quentin Christopher is still with us. We are in year five since he suffered the debilitating hemorrhagic stroke. We give God glory for His mercy and grace as Quentin remains in a skilled nursing facility where the Lord directs his care and recovery.

Finally, words are inadequate to express my appreciation to Mike Parker, my editor and publisher at WordCrafts Press. His compassion, faith in my abilities, and encouragement to keep at it brought this project to its conclusion. Thank you, Mike.

Beverly ND Clopton
March, 2022

Also by
Beverly ND Clopton

Rigors of the Call
Sonshine: Reflections of Faith
Surviving Pitfalls on the Path

Aslo Available from
WordCrafts Press

Finding God in the Bathroom
Dr. Brian Johnson

Pondering(s)
by Wayne Berry

Donkey Tales
by Keith Alexis

I AM
by Summer McKinney

What's the Big Idea?
by Robert G. Lee

www.wordcrafts.net

Lightning Source UK Ltd.
Milton Keynes UK
UKHW010633080223
416649UK00016B/700/J